Whole-of-Society Peacebuilding

The complex problems of peace, security, and development in societies affected by conflict increasingly demand innovative ideas, and comprehensive strategies to tackle the diverse, simultaneous, and daunting challenges faced in trying to rebuild states and communities after war. This comprehensive collection sets out a 'Whole-of-Society' (WoS) approach which focuses on the social contexts within which conflict resolution and prevention take place. The aim of WoS is to grasp the complexity both within local society and in the relations between external peacebuilders and the people they set out to help. The book argues that, by understanding multiple actors, their relationships, and the conditions in which they operate, complexity becomes an opportunity to be grasped, not simply an impediment to building peace.

This volume offers a novel perspective to advance and enrich debates on ownership of peace processes, resilience, hybridity, and liberal peacebuilding, and how these are influenced by local agency and social dynamics. Drawing on examples of conflicts in Ukraine, Mali, Yemen, Sri Lanka, Kosovo, and Georgia, the authors seek to address the operational gaps between interventions designed by outsiders and outcomes on the ground, suggesting how policymakers and civil society activists can achieve better configurations of external and local resources, delegate initiatives, and empower conflicted societies.

This book was originally published as a special issue of the journal *Peacebuilding*. Chapter 6 is available Open Access at https://www.routledge.com/products/9780367236885.

Mary Martin is a Senior Research Fellow at LSE IDEAS at the London School of Economics and Political Science, UK, where she directs the UN Business and Human Security Initiative. She is an Editor of the Routledge series *Studies in Human Security* and Co-Editor of the *Routledge Handbook of Human Security* (2014).

Vesna Bojicic-Dzelilovic is the Co-Director of the UN Business and Human Security Initiative at the London School of Economics and Political Science, UK. Her research focuses on the political economy of conflict and development. She is the co-author of *European Union in the Western Balkans: Hybrid Development, Hybrid Security and Hybrid Justice* (2018).

Whole-of-Society Peacebuilding

Edited by
Mary Martin and Vesna Bojicic-Dzelilovic

Routledge
Taylor & Francis Group
LONDON AND NEW YORK

First published 2019
by Routledge
2 Park Square, Milton Park, Abingdon, Oxon, OX14 4RN

and by Routledge
52 Vanderbilt Avenue, New York, NY 10017

Routledge is an imprint of the Taylor & Francis Group, an informa business

British Library Cataloguing-in-Publication Data
A catalogue record for this book is available from the British Library

ISBN13: 978-0-367-23688-5

Typeset in Minion Pro
by codeMantra

Publisher's Note
The publisher accepts responsibility for any inconsistencies that may have arisen during the conversion of this book from journal articles to book chapters, namely the inclusion of journal terminology.

Contents

Citation Information

The chapters in this book were originally published in the journal *Peacebuilding*, volume 6, issue 3 (September 2018). When citing this material, please use the original page numbering for each article, as follows:

Chapter 1

Mind the gaps. A Whole-of-Society approach to peacebuilding and conflict prevention
Mary Martin, Vesna Bojicic-Dzelilovic and Linda Benraïs
Peacebuilding, volume 6, issue 3 (September 2018) pp. 171–182

Chapter 2

From policy to action: assessing the European Union's approach to inclusive mediation and dialogue support in Georgia and Yemen
Véronique Dudouet, Alia Eshaq, Ekaterine Basilaia and Nana Macharashvili
Peacebuilding, volume 6, issue 3 (September 2018) pp. 183–200

Chapter 3

Decentralising power: building inclusive peace? The European Union's support to governance reform in Eastern Ukraine
Matteo Dressler
Peacebuilding, volume 6, issue 3 (September 2018) pp. 201–217

Chapter 4

Wholly local? ownership as philosophy and practice in peacebuilding interventions
Vesna Bojicic-Dzelilovic and Mary Martin
Peacebuilding, volume 6, issue 3 (September 2018) pp. 218–232

Chapter 5

Bracing the wind and riding the norm life cycle: inclusive peacebuilding in the European capacity building mission in Sahel–Mali (EUCAP Sahel–Mali)
Shyamika Jayasundara-Smits
Peacebuilding, volume 6, issue 3 (September 2018) pp. 233–247

Chapter 6

Coordinating international interventions in complex settings. An analysis of the EU peace and state-building efforts in post-independence Kosovo
Chris van der Borgh, Puck le Roy and Floor Zweerink
Peacebuilding, volume 6, issue 3 (September 2018) pp. 248–263

Chapter 7

Manoeuvring wars, rebels and governments: the EU's experience in Sri Lanka
Georg Frerks and Toon Dirkx
Peacebuilding, volume 6, issue 3 (September 2018) pp. 264–280

Notes on Contributors

Ekaterine Basilaia is a Researcher and a Lecturer at Ivane Javakhishvili Tbilisi State University, Georgia. She is a PhD Candidate in Media and Communication at Ivane Javakhishvili Tbilisi State University and the University of Antwerp, Belgium.

Linda Benraïs is an Adjunct Professor of Comparative Law and Mediation and the Director of the IRENE programme on Governance and Conflict Resolution at ESSEC Business School, France. Her research and publications focus on international negotiations, mediation, peacebuilding, and business ethics.

Vesna Bojicic-Dzelilovic is the Co-Director of the UN Business and Human Security Initiative at the London School of Economics and Political Science, UK. Her research focuses on the political economy of conflict and development.

Toon Dirkx is a PhD Candidate at the University of Basel, Switzerland, and a PhD Fellow at the swisspeace Statehood programme. His main research interests include the governance of armed groups in civil wars, and the interconnections between violence, interventionism, and state formation processes.

Matteo Dressler is a Researcher at the Flemish Peace Institute in Brussels working on issues of arms diversion in Europe and beyond. Before joining the Institute he was a Research Fellow for the Conflict Transformation Research Programme at Berghof Foundation in Berlin.

Véronique Dudouet is a Senior Researcher and the Programme Director at the Berghof Foundation, Berlin, Germany, where she manages collaborative research projects on non-state armed groups, negotiations, post-war governance, and civil resistance. She serves as a Co-Chair of the Academic Council of the International Center on Nonviolent Conflict, Washington, D.C., USA.

Alia Eshaq is an Entrepreneur and a Political Analyst. She is the Co-Founder of Pitchn, a group planning website. She used to work as a Researcher and Project Manager at the Berghof Foundation, Berlin, Germany.

Georg Frerks is a Professor. He holds a Chair in Conflict Prevention and Conflict Management at Utrecht University, the Netherlands, and a Chair in International Security Studies at the Netherlands Defence Academy. He focuses on contemporary intrastate conflicts and international and national conflict policies and interventions, often with a focus on Sri Lankan conflict.

Shyamika Jayasundara-Smits is an Assistant Professor of Conflict and Peace Studies at the International Institute of Social Studies (ISS) of Erasmus University Rotterdam, the Netherlands. She also teaches in Governance and Conflict in ISS's Master of Arts Degree Programme in Development Studies.

Puck le Roy has worked with the European Commission and as a Policy Officer at the Dutch Embassy, Berlin, Germany.

Nana Macharashvili is an Associate Professor in the Department of Political Science at Ivane Javakhishvili Tbilisi State University (TSU), Georgia. She is also the Director of the Interdisciplinary Center, and the Head of the Master of Arts Programme in Public Policy and Administration at TSU. She is actively involved in the training programmes dedicated to participatory policy planning.

Mary Martin is a Senior Research Fellow at LSE IDEAS at the London School of Economics and Political Science, UK, where she directs the UN Business and Human Security Initiative. She is an Editor of the Routledge series *Studies in Human Security*.

Chris van der Borgh is an Assistant Professor, a Lecturer, a Researcher, and a Consultant with the Centre for Conflict Studies at Utrecht University, the Netherlands. He specialises in issues of peace and security, political order, and international intervention.

Floor Zweerink is a Researcher in the field of International Security at the Ministry of Justice and Security in the Netherlands.

Mind the gaps. A Whole-of-Society approach to peacebuilding and conflict prevention

Mary Martin, Vesna Bojicic-Dzelilovic and Linda Benraïs

ABSTRACT

External peacebuilding interventions have moved towards comprehensive strategies to tackle the complex problems of peace, security and development. This paper proposes a 'Whole-of-Society' (WOS) approach which seeks to enhance the effectiveness of externally led peacebuilding and conflict prevention through recourse to the social contexts within which they are implemented. The aim of WOS is to see complexity, both within local society and in the relations between external peacebuilders and local society, as an opportunity to be grasped, as much as an impediment to effective outcomes. A WOS approach adds a practice dimension to debates on ownership, local peace and hybridity, trust-in-peacebuilding and their conceptualisations of local agency and dynamics. It seeks to address the operational gaps that emerge within a societal perspective to peacebuilding, in particular by suggesting ways of achieving appropriate configurations of external and local resources, agency and initiatives.

A recurrent theme in conflict and security studies is the integration of discrete concepts and policy actions in order to achieve a more rounded and, by implication, a more effective response to situations of violence and instability, delivered by external intervention. This has led to pairing security and development, the synthesis of civilian and military capabilities and combinations of global, regional and local initiatives, as examples of how peacebuilding discourse has tended to bundle together otherwise standalone components.[1] In part, this trend reflects a need to deal with the increasing breadth and complexity of current conflict environments. Single approaches no longer seem adequate to the task.[2] Holistic approaches recognise a multiplicity of security needs and competing priorities for external attention, while comprehensive strategies seek to construct overarching programmes out of diverse elements such as

---

[1]Theo Neethling, 'The Security-Development Nexus and the Imperative of Peacebuilding with Special Reference to the African Context', *African Journal on Conflict Resolution* 5, no. 1 (2005): 33–60; Shyamika Jayasundara-Smits, *Civil-Military Synergies at Operational Level in EU External Action* (The Hague: Global Partnership for the Prevention of Armed Conflict, 2016); Marco Paulino Serronha, Optimization of Civil-Military Synergies in the Field of Crisis Management, Nação e Defesa, Nº 129 – 5.ª Série, 129–143.

[2]Robert Ricigliano, 'Networks of Effective Action: Implementing an Integrated Approach to Peacebuilding', *Security Dialogue* 34, no. 4 (2003): 445–462.

administrative and technical experience, combat troops, diplomats and civil servants, judges and lawyers and development economists, all of which may be appropriate, but only some of which may be relevant to the specific circumstances of each conflict, and each intervention, thus setting up dilemmas of selection. The consequence for theory and practice of this trend towards comprehensiveness and the ability to choose from multiple components is that the problematic of peacebuilding interventions is framed in terms of the political and technical difficulties of combination and integration and how to manage an unwieldy process of many moving parts.[3] Such a challenge suggests a supply-side, or 'inside-out' logic, reinforced by 'self-referential' paradigms that govern the design of external intervention policies,[4] in which intervening states and international organisations grapple with how to implement their own policy choices and deploy variegated toolkits.[5] As has been noted, particularly in critical security studies, this perspective tends to relegate the needs, wishes and perspectives of conflict-affected societies.[6]

This special issue frames the challenge posed to external peacebuilding as one of complex and dense conflict environments. Its aim is to suggest possibilities for combining diverse elements, actors and processes. Our approach is pragmatic, proposing that the need is for operational guidance as much as theories of change or new concepts of security. We have attempted to articulate 'Whole-of-Society' (WOS) as a practice-based approach which seeks to enhance the effectiveness of externally led peacebuilding and conflict prevention through recourse to the social contexts within which they are implemented, and with the aim of seeing complexity, within local society and in the relations between external peacebuilders and local society, as an opportunity to be grasped, as much as an impediment to effective outcomes.

WOS proposes a thicker form of engagement between external policies and conflict-affected societies, while recognising that in common with all peacebuilding approaches, this does not offer immediate solutions and may indeed raise further challenges and barriers in terms of efficiency and legitimacy. Thicker engagement requires identification of and systematic involvement with the breadth and diversity of actors which operate at multiple levels related to the conflict environment, from states and international

[3]Cedric de Coning and Karsten Friis, 'Coherence and Coordination, The Limits of the Comprehensive Approach', *Journal of International Peacekeeping* 15, no. 1–2 (2011): 243–272; Michael Zürn and Anna Herrhausen, 'Post-Conflict Peacebuilding: The Roles of Ownership and Coordination', in *Strategies for Peace. Contributions of International Organizations, States and Non-State Actors*, ed. Volker Rittberger and Martina Fischer (Opladen & Farmington Hills: Barbara Budrich Publishers, 2008), 271–287; Roland Paris, 'Understanding the "Coordination Problem" in Postwar Statebuilding' in *The Dilemmas of Statebuilding: Confronting the Contradictions of Postwar Peace Operations*, ed. Roland Paris and Timothy D. Sisk (Abingdon, Oxfordshire: Routledge, 2009), 53–78.

[4]Tobias Debiel and Daniel Lambach (2009) 'How State-Building Strategies Miss Local Realities', *Peace Review* 21, no. 1 (2009): 22.

[5]Damien Helly, Greta Galeazzi, Asmita Parshotam, Cecilia Gregersen, Willy Kokolo and Andrew Sherriff, A. (2015). Stepping up? Best Practice in Joint Programming and Prospects for EU Joint Cooperation Strategies. Maastricht: ECDPM.

[6]Roger Mac Ginty and Oliver P Richmond, 'The Local Turn in Peace Building: A Critical Agenda for Peace', *Third World Quarterly* 34, no. 5 (2013): 763–783; Vivienne Jabri, 'Peacebuilding, the Local and the International: A Colonial or a Postcolonial Rationality?', *Peacebuilding* 1, no. 1 (2013): 3–16; Tania Paffenholz, *Civil Society and Peacebuilding. A Critical Assessment* (Boulder: Lynne Rienner Publishers, 2010); .Kristoffer Lidén, 'Building Peace between Global and Local Politics: The Cosmopolitical Ethics of Liberal Peacebuilding', *International Peacekeeping* 16, no. 5 (2009): 616–634; Astri Suhrke, 'The Dangers of a Tight Embrace: Externally Assisted Statebuilding in Afghanistan' in *The Dilemmas of Statebuilding: Confronting the Contradictions of Postwar Peace Operations*, ed. Roland Paris and Timothy D. Sisk (London and New York: Routledge, 2009), 227–251; Roland Paris, 'International Peacebuilding and the "Mission Civilisatrice"', *Review of International Studies* 28, no. 4 (2002): 638.

institutions, global civil society, to local actors, as well as the existence of numerous relationships at policy level and on the ground. WOS proposes that interventions take account of not only actors in the conflict space, but also of formal and informal processes through which actors relate to each other and respond to conflict. It is through practitioners exploring and exploiting the detail of this dense kaleidoscope of actors and actorness that WOS envisages the emergence of fresh perspectives regarding working in the conflict space and the development of improved capacities. As the article on local ownership in this issue highlights, several things are going on here: externals must navigate multiple local dynamics and highly variegated socio-political orders; different perceptions exist of the conflict at every level from the international to the grass roots and the combination of externals and locals creates a contested arena of perspectives and interests. Interaction is rarely straightforward and constitutes a dynamic of its own that adds a further dimension beyond consideration of peacebuilding as driven by (either) external/or local factors.[7] Against this backdrop, partnership and co-operation are not necessarily 'difficult'.[8] There is also the possibility of creative interactions between outsiders and insiders as well as within each of these categories. Thus, the question we consider here is not only how to limit the hazards of complex interaction but how to realise its potential.

WOS does not argue for an expansive vision of peacebuilding that implies additional policies, outreach to more actors or require externals to work with every civil society group. 'Whole' is not synonymous with 'all'. The aim is not to simply increase the scope of intervention in a potentially infinite extension of inclusivity and comprehensiveness. More comprehensiveness and inclusivity may be neither feasible nor effective and risk diluting rather than improving the appropriateness of external action. Instead, the ability to define priorities and comparative advantages, and work with the fabric of local society based on a more profound understanding of context and changes in context, is proposed as part of a granular approach, which allows external actors to manoeuvre effectively and in a targeted way in complex settings.

As Schirch notes, the relationships between peacebuilding actors, the factors driving and mitigating conflict and activities taking place in different sectors comprise an 'ecological relationship' characterised by interdependence.[9] A WOS approach emphasises the importance of understanding the totality rather than discrete elements of conflict and responses to it, but it also problematises the nature of interdependence and the perverse and positive relational dynamics which are triggered by conflict and its aftermath. This seeks to recast policy design, implementation and adaptation not as technical aspects of realising external interventions, but to ground them in the sociology of conflict and intervention, which is specific to each conflict situation.

A WOS approach sits within a scholarly discourse which brings a societal perspective to peacebuilding, regarding it as an activity rooted in political, social, cultural, economic and technological processes and the characteristics of the

[7]Christian Lotz, 'International Norms in Statebuilding: Finding a Pragmatic Approach. *Global Governance*', 16, no.2 (2010): 220, 232.
[8]Debiel and Lambach, 'How State-Building Strategies', 24.
[9]Lisa Schirch, 'Where Does Whole of Government Meet Whole-of-Society?' in *Conflict Management and 'Whole of Government'*, ed. Volker C. Franke and Robert H. Dorf (Carlisle, United States: Strategic Studies Institute of the US Army War College, 2012), 463.

conflict-affected society, including indigenous norms and practices.[10] Its premise is that governance interventions based on local realities, traditions and culture are preferable to state-building projects focusing primarily on creating new institutions.[11] WOS adds a practice dimension to debates on ownership, local peace and hybridity, trust-in-peacebuilding and their conceptualisations of local agency and dynamics as significant to the outcomes of intervention.[12] However, rather than arguing solely within these lines of scholarly discussion or even proposing more ethnological perspectives[13] in a bid to improve the authenticity of practice, WOS seeks to contribute to finding ways of implementing peace and state-building as a societal enterprise and for re-imagining the possibilities created by external intervention.

A societal turn can also be seen in policy discourses which seek to analyse deep-seated conditions within conflict-affected societies and address peacebuilding with mechanisms of social reform, ranging from governance to health, education and environmental management.[14] The idea of WOS emerges from 'Whole of Government' and joined-up government in public administration, which became popular during the early 2000s.[15] Here, the proposition is that a heterogeneity of stakeholders, collaborative working and the diffusion/reassembling of responsibilities[16] and 'boundary crossing' initiatives between different practice perspectives can be seen as significant as working through classic organisational structures.[17] The supposed benefit is to create space for autonomous, peripheral actions while improving connectivity and co-ordination between diverse components, actors and processes.[18]

In the context of peacebuilding (as distinct from public administration), this definition suggests similarities between the WOS approach and the trend towards resilience building with its focus on individuals at grass-roots (whether beneficiaries or providers of security) and implies a proposal to transform rather than simply preserve the social status quo through a multilevel, multidimensional and

[10]Beatrice Pouligny, Civil Society and Post-Conflict Peacebuilding: Ambiguities of International Programmes Aimed at Building 'New' Societies. *Security Dialogue*, 36, no.4 (2005), 496.

[11]Anna K. Jarstad and Roberto Belloni, 'Introducing Hybrid Peace Governance: Impact and Prospects of Liberal Peacebuilding', *Global Governance* 18, no. 1 (2012): 1–6; Michael G Dillon and Julian Reid, 'Complex Political Emergencies, Global Governance and Liberal Peace', *Alternatives* 25, no. 1 (2000): 117–14; Volker Boege et al., 'Building Peace and Political Community in Hybrid Political Orders', *International Peacekeeping* 16, no. 5 (2009): 599–615.

[12]Roberto Belloni, 'Hybrid Peace Governance: Its Emergence and Significance', *Global Governance* 18, no. 1 (2012): 21–38; Roger Mac Ginty, 'Hybrid Peace: The Interaction between Top Down and Bottom Up Peace', *Security Dialogue* 41, no. 4 (2010): 391–412; Roger Mac Ginty, *International Peacebuilding and Local Resistance: Hybrid Forms of Peace* (Basingstoke, UK: Palgrave Macmillan, 2011); Sonja Grimm, 'External Democratization after War: Success and Failure'. *Democratisation*, 15, no3 (2008), 537.

[13]Birgit Bräuchler and Philipp Naucke, 'Peacebuilding and Conceptualisations of the Local', *Social Anthropology* 25, no. 4 (2017): 422–436.

[14]Institute for Economics and Peace, *Positive Peace Report* (2017), 3, http://visionofhumanity.org/app/uploads/2017/10/Positive-Peace-Report-2017.pdf
[accessed 29 January, 2018].

[15]Tom Christensen and Per Laegreid, The Whole-of-Government Approach to Public Sector Reform *Public Administration Review*, 67, no.6 (2007),1059.

[16]Ilona Kickbush and David Gleicher, 'Governance for Health in the 21st Century' (Copenhagen: World Health Organisation 2012).

[17]Simon Chesterman, Michael Ignatieff and Ramesh Thakur, *Making States Work. State Failure and the Crisis of Governance* (Tokyo: United Nations University Press 2005), 1.

[18]Schirch, 'Where Does Whole of', 463.

multilateral approach,[19] which joins together all sectors with a possible link to peace and development. Resilience building is also premised on deepening relations between policymakers and a diverse array of civil society institutions including 'cultural organisations, religious communities, social partners, human rights defenders' and the private sector as partners.[20]

In policy terms, WOS is part of a trajectory in intervention which has moved from attempting to pacify conflict societies through military and coercive means, towards an emphasis on stabilisation and reform measures, and in a further step, the co-production of peace, the creation of resilience and organic interaction between multiple external and internal stakeholders, including so-called hybrid peace formulations. As part of the cognitive shift from seeing intervention as predominantly externally driven, towards a recognition of the local, the proposition of *WOS* is that peacebuilding and conflict prevention will be more effective if they are enacted as social and relational processes, and when a range of actors, actions and intentions are identified and taken into account. In this vein, the motivation for a WOS approach is to address the practice gaps that emerge from a societal perspective and suggest ways of achieving appropriate configurations of external and local resources, agency and initiatives.

Rather than simply following a generalised 'local turn' in peacebuilding with its emphases on the acceptance/acceptability of externally led reforms, and in gaining a more accurate picture of indigenous agency,[21] WOS proposes a disaggregation of the local into salient constituencies of actor and agency, where this salience is context specific, and prescribes actions informed by strategic combinations of actors and processes. It emphasises a relational dimension, seeing peacebuilding as an inherently interactive process animated by the resources, capacities and perspectives of both local society and external actors. If the motivation for a WOS approach is complexity of the peacebuilding environment, the nature of complexity can be understood as not only comprising multiple agents and forms of agency, but also constant shifts in conditions on the ground and the need for continuous review and reshaping of relations and engagements between people and processes.

In terms of policy utility, rather than proposing WOS as a novel concept to reframe the goals and methods of civilian peacebuilding, the premise in this special issue is that it can sharpen and refine what external actors do in applying comprehensive approaches and engaging in deep-seated interventions which disrupt in profound ways the local social fabric, for example with governance and security reform measures. The aim here is that WOS can offer new purpose and traction to these sensitive and difficult initiatives.

We have used the case of EU interventions in conflict and crisis settings to propose and examine the principal characteristics of a WOS approach; to provide empirical insights into how it could add value by looking at specific examples of EU policies in

[19]European Commission, *Shared Vision, Common Action: A Stronger Europe. A Global Strategy for the European Union's Foreign And Security Policy* (2016), 25, 27, 28, http://www.mfa.gov.rs/eugs_review_web.pdf [accessed 29 January 2018]; European Commission, *Joint Communication to the European Parliament and the Council – A Strategic Approach to Resilience in the EU's External Action* (2017), (JOIN(2017) 21 final).

[20]European Commission, *Shared Vision*, 27.

[21]Mac Ginty and Richmond, 'The Local Turn in Peace Building', 766; Oliver P Richmond, 'A Post-Liberal Peace: Eirenism and the Everyday', *Review of International Studies* 35, no. 3 (2009): 557–580; Timothy Donais, 'Empowerment or Imposition? Dilemmas of Local Ownership in Post-Conflict Peacebuilding Processes', *Peace & Change* 34, no. 1 (2009): 3–26; Oliver P Richmond, 'Resistance and the Post-Liberal Peace', *Millennium: Journal of International Studies* 38, no. 3 (2010): 665–692.

action; and also to consider critically its limitations. Comprehensiveness is a distinctive feature of the EU's global role in conflict and crisis management, representing 'a [] working method and a set of concrete measures and processes to improve how the EU, based on a common strategic vision and drawing on its wide array of existing tools and instruments, collectively can develop, embed and deliver more coherent and more effective policies, working practices, actions and results'.[22]

With the launch of the EU Global Security Strategy (EUGSS) in June 2016, and in its Council Conclusions of January 2018, the EU emphasised integration as a core feature of its external action with the aim of improving inclusiveness and efficiency. The Integrated Approach refers to multilevel applications of policies and instruments which 'respect[s] and reaffirm[s] the various mandates, roles, aims and legal frameworks of the stakeholders involved'.[23] Both documents (the EUGSS and the Council Conclusions) signal a desire to go beyond the Comprehensive Approach and not only address issues of technical co-ordination but develop a common orientation towards citizens as the glue for improved coherence between policies.[24] Thus, the social environment is constituted as a focus of external action,[25] although the practical detail of a citizen orientation remains largely unspecified in EU policy texts. In the EUGSS, the referent environment is mainly European society, although gearing action towards citizens implies increased accountability and transparency towards destination as well as European publics.[26] Commitments to use public resources for peacebuilding and conflict prevention effectively and tailor policy decisions to (a broadly defined) public interest add detail to this civic vision of external action, but practice changes such as new measures for accountability, transparency and popular legitimacy will be needed to deliver on this citizen focus. Accountability (itself a contested terrain of policy)[27] may in fact add a novel dimension to and thicken the engagement between external and local societies, for example, if the demands of 'sending' populations (such as European publics, particularly to export international norms as part of external relations) shape interventionist behaviour towards 'receiving' countries.[28]

Such interactions between societies bound up in the practice of external peacebuilding underline the salience of the idea of using 'Whole of Society' to capture how interventions become a societal enterprise across borders. WOS can also be seen as part of an enhanced capabilities approach, with interventions aligned more closely to the relative capacities of both external actors and local populations. EU capabilities have been conceptualised as the capability to act, fund, co-ordinate and co-operate. Thus, they depend primarily on the availability of European personnel, materiel and experience.[29] A WOS approach proposes

[22]Council of the European Union, *Council Conclusions on the EU's Comprehensive Approach* (2014), 1, http://www.consilium.europa.eu/uedocs/cms_Data/docs/pressdata/EN/foraff/142552.pdf [accessed 28 January 2018].

[23]Council of the European Union, *Council Conclusions on the Integrated Approach to External Conflicts and Crises* (2018), 2, https://ec.europa.eu/europeaid/sites/devco/files/2018-01-cnl_conclusions_on_ia.pdf [accessed 28 January 2018].

[24]European Commission, *Shared Vision*, 9, 28.

[25]European Commission, *Shared Vision*, 5, 8, 14, 29.

[26]European Commission, *Shared Vision*, 31, 51.

[27]Perspectives on the Peacebuilding Commission and Mutual Accountability, *International Peace Institute, Issue Brief*, November 2009, 1–2.

[28]Lotz 'International Norms in Statebuilding', 228.

[29]Richard G Whitman and Stefan Wolff, (2012) *The European Union as a Global Conflict Manager*, New York: Routledge, 2012.

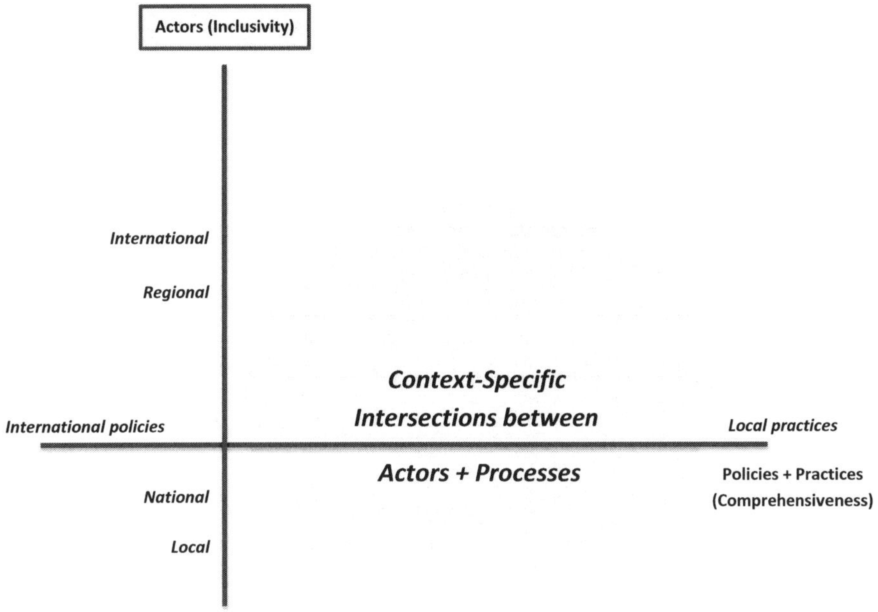

Figure 1. Whole-of-Society approach.

that EU capabilities are partly a function of how these resources are deployed in the context of receiving populations and of how they can be integrated with indigenous capacities.[30]

The implications of this shift in emphasis on the ground in conflict-affected societies are to require continuous and systematic identifications and analysis of context, in terms of actor groups, perceptions and expectations as well as the crafting of shared understandings about the aims and remit of policies as part of policy design and adaptation. An important aspect of an engagement strategy is to access 'inactive publics', namely local constituencies that for a variety of reasons remain out of the purview of EU standard practices. Here again, while the focus is on overlooked elements within target populations in conflict countries, there is a 'feedback loop' to external actors. The idea of inactive and invisible publics came out of a literature which looked at western societies and their hidden capacities for action within the sphere of democratic politics.[31] In this sense, WOS could also be a way of mobilising latent constituencies within intervening countries. It should not suggest that effort is only needed in mining the depth and extent of conflict-affected society. We have visualised a WOS approach in terms of a grid that includes two axes (Figure 1). The vertical axis represents an actor perspective and here both the normative and practical/operational challenge is to improve inclusivity and engage a wide range of actors in peacebuilding interventions. These actors exist at multiple levels from the international down to the local. They may be connected in different degrees, times and spatial dimensions. They

[30]Chris van der Borgh, Mary Martin and Vesna Bojicic-Dzelilovic, *EU Capabilities in Conflict Prevention and Peacebuilding: Challenges, Strengths and Opportunities of a Whole-of-Society Approach*, WOSCAP, 31 May 2017, P8; http://www.woscap.eu/documents/131298403/131299900/Research+Report.pdf/8469fddb-06c5-46c0-aa14-d7a32eb13cc5.

[31]Darren Brunk, '"Whole-of-Society" Peacebuilding: A New Approach for Forgotten Stakeholders', *International Journal* 71, no. 1 (2015): 1–26.

may be active or passive and have highly articulated or implicit interests and agendas. Categories and levels of actors can be further disaggregated to reveal multiple groups and different layers of interests, capacities and power. Networked relations between them are important in assessing not only how relevant they are to a particular field of peacebuilding practice, how they might behave towards issues such as reform and conflict resolution, the multiplier effects to be considered from their interactions, but also how their agency is realised through particular processes, practices and policies. For this reason, the vertical axis is not only about inclusivity, but has to be seen in conjunction with the horizontal axis which visualises ways in which groups and individuals, whether local, regional or international, act in the conflict space.

The horizontal axis comprises multiple actions located in different fields of practice and policy. It represents possibilities for a comprehensive approach, through offering different entry points where an external actor can choose to intervene through engaging with local processes or by introducing its own policies and initiatives. Context will limit the actual possibilities from a potentially infinite number to a realistic and actually existing number of options which include both those generated by local actors, those which are part of the intervener's 'toolkit' and those undertaken by other external third parties.

All the studies in this special issue underline the reality of how this conjunction of multiple actors and actions characterises and shapes conflict spaces and determines the practical outcomes of intervention. In the case of European Union interventions, the impression is that complexity is a hurdle to be overcome, and efforts under rubrics such as local ownership, coherence and integration are partly about making the best of a difficult job. Practice and scholarly literature on these subjects tend in similar directions.[32] Certainly, the studies suggest that logics of choice about the nature, timing and method of action or who to work with and include is not clearly conceptualised or communicated. It is against the backdrop of this evidence that the authors propose different ways of using WOS to enhance EU interventions.

The studies are based on a two-year research project for the European Commission which assessed the EU's capabilities for civilian conflict prevention and peacebuilding, including detailed case studies of intervention policies in Yemen, Ukraine, Mali and Georgia as well as reviewing practice examples in other locations such as Sri Lanka, Afghanistan and Kosovo.[33]

The first two papers illustrate the challenges of comprehensiveness and inclusivity from the vantage point of policies on multi-track diplomacy and governance reform, looking at specific examples from EU interventions in Yemen, Georgia and Ukraine. Here, we can see how a WOS approach can work as both an analytical and operational complement, which makes visible the gaps and tensions in working with multi-actor and multilevel policy parameters. In terms of the vertical axis and the benefits of inclusivity, Dudouet et al. in their article on multi-track diplomacy show how a WOS approach to mediation and dialogue could move away from a reliance on elite bargaining towards interactions with

[32]Lotz, 'International Norms in Peacebuilding', 231; Isabell Schierenbeck, 'Beyond the Local Turn Divide: Lessons Learned, Relearnt and Unlearnt'. *Third World Quarterly* 36, no.5 (2015): 1023–1032; Gearoid Millar, 'Expectations and Experiences of Peacebuilding in Sierra Leone: Parallel Peacebuilding Processes and Compound Friction', *International Peacekeeping* 20, no2 (2013): 189–203; 'Ole Jacob Sending, Why Peacebuilders Fail to Secure Ownership and be Sensitive to Context'. (*NUPI Working Paper 755*. Oslo: Norwegian Institute for International Affairs, 2009).

[33]Whole-of-Society Conflict Prevention and Peacebuilding (WOSCAP). Further details and findings from the research are available at www.woscap.eu.

multiple conflict stakeholders and affected constituencies with the aim of improving the sustainability of agreements and contributing to the democratisation of peace processes. Specifically, this requires emphasising the roles of and relations with local actors beyond the central state level, including civil society organisations, women, youths, religious actors and minority groups (e.g. regional, cultural, religious, linguistic or ethnic communities), that have been historically excluded or marginalised from this kind of process. Their examination of multi-track diplomacy in Yemen suggests possibilities of the vertical axis to identify outlier groups and improve inclusivity in a field of intervention which historically has been limited to a select group of stakeholders. At the same time, the authors use WOS as an analytical lens to explore issues such as thetensions that arise between increased participation on the one hand and the effectiveness of peace processes on the other. Can a WOS approach help strike a balance between the quantitative levels of participation and the quality of inputs through involving different groups of stakeholders and identifying and cultivating synergies between points on the horizontal axis (which could affect the timing or nature of action)? An obvious impediment to vertical inclusivity is tension between different groups of local actors and the spoiler or exclusionary behaviours of constituencies towards those it regards as rivals – for power or external assistance. A WOS approach increases the likelihood of external interveners having to regulate such encounters and deal with the possibility of embracing one or more groups as collaborators at the expense of others. At the same time, it is possible that a WOS approach may help make such dilemmas visible in order to tackle them, where traditional approaches towards target populations which rely largely on elite contacts may occlude them.

Similarly, one challenge posed by the use of the horizontal axis could be disjunctures between different policy goals. Moreover, integrating multiple actor constituencies with the deployment of diverse forms of action may bring intervention closer to the actual nature and operational reality of local society but at the expense of creating clear lines of accountability and responsibility.

In his paper on EU support for decentralisation in Ukraine as an example of governance reform interventions, Dressler also uses WOS as an analytical device to look at linkages between multiple actors affected by and able to affect the outcome of a contentious process. Here, the vertical axis serves to reveal salient connections between diverse stakeholders and the horizontal axis to highlight potential synergies and co-ordination between different policy fields relevant in the reform process. Contacts and working relationships were critical for mobilising local support, to reform and develop a sophisticated database and for understanding of key actors and processes which supported the capabilities of external actors to act in this area. Dressler shows that WOS is not just about illuminating opportunities for policy effectiveness in multi-actor, multi-process environments. It has a critical value in that it questions the assumption that increased co-ordination and inclusivity by themselves will necessarily deliver improved outcomes. In a constructive sense, WOS becomes a useful device for (re)viewing what co-ordination and inclusivity look like in practice.

The next two papers zoom in more closely on the normative aspirations implicit in EU interventions, including attempts to improve citizen participation in reform processes as well as encourage greater inclusivity as part of the outcomes they deliver. Papers on local ownership by Bojicic-Dzelilovic and Martin and on EU-led security sector reform in Mali by Jayasundera provide examples of the limitations of norm implementation in EU policies. Both papers provide a critical assessment of what the

EU has been able to achieve and gaps between its normative claims and actual practice. In the case of local ownership, the authors look at the possibilities for accessing outlier constituencies, such as business and faith groups, to improve local participation and for leveraging indigenous initiatives and forms of association. In the case of Ukraine, highly fluid forms of mobilisation and activist networks assisted by social media began with the Maidan revolution. Whether undertaken by NGOs, business networks or religious movements, these citizen initiatives are connected to wider networks of activists and victims than are typically accessed by EU policies or funds. Small and sometimes informally organised groups track the rapidly changing dynamics and shifting public attitudes towards the conflict, which are at odds with more static EU strategies. Through these groups, we can see the benefits and outlines of a thicker form of engagement, which could translate 'local ownership' from an ideal into a constructive system of collaboration between externals and locals.

Jayasundera's analysis of the EUCAP-Sahel mission to Mali is another example of the EU's tendency towards functional interventions where a normative edge has been blunted by a perceived tension between effectiveness and norms, as well as the EU's choice to emphasise the technical nature of the mission, in order to play down its political implications. Here, we see a possible contradiction in the priorities of EU external action, between 'principled pragmatism' which is explicit in the case of the EUCAP-Sahel mission and the EU's historic adherence to norms such as local ownership and gender equality. In the Mali case, local ownership and inclusivity were limited in both the training and outreach activities of the mission. However, excluding cadres who interact with populations at community level, those in the North of the country and women's groups meant missed opportunities to learn from their knowledge of local security needs, and to map onto local processes, to the detriment of both the relevance of the mission and the achievement of normative outcomes such as building trust, confidence and legitimacy of security institutions. A similar tension was evident in the case of the EU's multi-track diplomacy in Yemen where pragmatic engagement with elites risked overshadowing its explicit support for gender equality.

The final two papers move from individual policy examples to country-wide interventions in conflict where the EU attempts to deploy a range of tools from diplomacy to justice and trade. The examples of Kosovo and Sri Lanka show the constraints on comprehensiveness where both effectiveness and normative ambition become compromised by the EU's inability to manoeuvre strategically despite having recourse to multiple different instruments. In Kosovo, these included specific initiatives on governance reform through the EULEX Mission, the Stabilisation and Association process and political dialogue. As Van der Borgh states, there is no other country where the EU has played such a central role in the process of state building and stabilisation. Despite an apparently strong capability to act, and even its readiness to adapt interventions and shift between policies in order to react to the changing situation in the country, the EU was hampered by an inability to diversify ownership of the state-building process and its unsatisfactory relationship with uncooperative state elites. Van der Borgh uses the case to show the relevance of capabilities in context rather than as an abstract set of resources, where the ability to act, adapt, co-ordinate and fund could be reinforced through a more explicit WOS approach in order to contextualise relationships and policy options and include a broader range of stakeholders beyond the government level.

In complex contexts, such as Sri Lanka and Kosovo, the difficulties in applying a WOS approach may be considerable. One of the aims of this special issue is to not only demonstrate how WOS can add value to what is already being done, but also be critical about its proposition. In their paper, Frerks and Dirkx show how the shrinking space for civil society in Sri Lanka reduced the visibility and impact of the EU's intervention and undermined its goals of bringing a range of policies to bear on the humanitarian, political and economic challenges of the conflict. Despite an extensive and increasing involvement in the country since 2002, the influence of the EU and other external parties involved diminished as local actors and dynamics, particularly government policies, squeezed out both civil society and international engagement, resulting in what the authors describe as 'an unpredictable and volatile experience leading to setbacks and outright failures' including the internationally supported peace process itself. Despite a large repertoire of instruments, the EU found itself overwhelmed by the intractability of the conflict, the lack of local buy-in and the spoiler behaviour of important constituencies and of the protagonist parties. Both comprehensiveness of action and engagement with local actors were stymied, while the EU lost traction with the government. Only after a change of government was the EU able to regain leverage, especially through its use of trade conditionalities. At the national level, the EU's inclusivity and use of civilian space were seriously affected by the adverse conditions, although individual NGOs and CSOs found EU support very valuable, if not essential for their continued operations. This points to two conclusions – the first about the difficulties of applying a WOS approach in the face of resistance and restricted opportunities, but second about the need for a strategy which would allow the EU to deploy and manoeuvre under adverse conditions more effectively, applying its tools such as funding, trade and diplomacy in a targeted way, and adapting to setbacks in policy objectives.

The findings of the individual papers suggest issue-specific as well as collective lessons for peacebuilding theory and practice. They are not conclusive about how a WOS approach might work or even its ultimate value. In presenting them, our aim is to offer an initial conceptualisation which can be reviewed in the light of further empirical evidence. The studies provide different perspectives on current practice debates about external assistance for peacebuilding, illustrating some of the challenges faced in complex actor environments. They highlight the ways in which even an actor that directs its strategy towards delivering comprehensive solutions and seeks to promote global norms, as publicly as the EU does, and engages actively with local society to enlarge civil spaces, still can fail to achieve some of its principal objectives. By reviewing a range of policy interventions, and highlighting strategic goals such as ownership and inclusivity, we hope to suggest why and how a WOS approach might address some of the shortcomings encountered in the EU case. Common patterns emerge across the papers, such as tensions between the technical functionality of interventions compared with the deeply political nature of particular policies such as decentralisation in Ukraine, the justice reforms of the EULEX Kosovo mission and efforts at gender inclusivity in the Yemen National Dialogue. Inclusivity also has its limits as the evidence from EU actions in Yemen, Kosovo, Mail and Ukraine suggests, with the EU either failing to go beyond a superficial engagement with local actors – the problem of 'usual suspects' -or finding it difficult to sustain inclusivity over time and under pressure whether from the acuity of conflict or exclusionary behaviour on the part of local elites. The aim here is to be constructively critical of external interventions, hence the suggestion to see WOS as an immanent capability of EU actorness grounded in what it already does. The examples in this issue suggest that there is will and resource on the part of the EU for an authentic engagement, with among others, women peacebuilders and small civil society groups and for striking a better balance between these elements of society and the dominance of elite voices, but that practice in this area can be refined, sharpened and embedded.

This special issue also attempts to supplement a wider research agenda that engages with and illuminates the societal dimensions of peacebuilding. As such we present preliminary ideas for further investigating the multifaceted nature of conflict society, and how externally led state and peacebuilding can engage with it, which we hope others will follow.

Disclosure statement

No potential conflict of interest was reported by the authors.

Funding

The research for the article was conducted as part of the project Whole of Society Conflict Prevention and Peacebuilding (WOSCAP), funded by the EU's Horizon 2020 Research and Innovation Programme, Grant agreement no. 653866 and European Commission [653866].

ORCID

Linda Benraïs http://orcid.org/0000-0002-5134-356X

From policy to action: assessing the European Union's approach to inclusive mediation and dialogue support in Georgia and Yemen

Véronique Dudouet, Alia Eshaq, Ekaterine Basilaia and Nana Macharashvili

ABSTRACT

This paper examines the opportunities and challenges of a Whole-of-Society approach to peacebuilding through the prism of EU multi-track diplomacy in conflict-affected environments. Although inclusivity has emerged as a global normative imperative embedded in various international policy guidelines, the literature on inclusive political settlements highlights that participatory processes do not necessarily contribute to effective decision-making outcomes. The paper assesses how EU actors seek to overcome this dilemma when supporting mediation and dialogue processes in third countries, and how local actors assess such interventions. Through a comparative review of EU intervention in Georgia and Yemen, the paper argues that multi-track mediation and dialogue support might provide an effective strategy to promote a meaningful participation by all relevant stakeholders in peace processes, but only if adequate mechanisms for inter-track coordination are provided for, and if vertical multi-actor inclusivity is complemented by horizontal coherence between diplomatic action and other policy domains of intervention.

Introduction

In November 2009, the Council of the European Union adopted a 'Concept on Strengthening EU Mediation and Dialogue Capacities', as part of its efforts to implement the 2003 European Security Strategy. This document reflected, among other priorities, the wish to employ mediation and dialogue in a holistic and inclusive fashion by pursuing 'both a top-down and a bottom-up approach in parallel tracks, which reinforce and inform each other'.[1] This statement reflected a growing ambition by the EU – alongside other international organisations – to promote inclusivity as the norm of engagement for peacebuilding interventions in war-affected or post-war contexts. Nearly a decade later, do the current capacities of EU institutions in the field of mediation and dialogue match these ambitious

---

[1]Council of the European Union, *Council/Commission Joint Concept on strengthening EU mediation and dialogue capacities*, 15,779/09 (10 November 2009). See online at: http://eeas.europa.eu/cfsp/conflict_prevention/docs/concept_strengthening_eu_med_en.pdf.

normative ideals? And more importantly, in the context of this special issue, how does EU diplomatic engagement in conflicts beyond its borders illustrate the opportunities and challenges of whole-of-society peacebuilding efforts?

This paper aims to assess the nature and dimensions of EU multi-track diplomatic engagement from the specific perspective of vertical state-society inclusivity, which represents one of the two axes of the Whole-of-Society (WOS) perspective investigated in this special issue as a promising lens to analyse peacebuilding and conflict prevention strategies. A WOS approach to mediation and dialogue implies that transforming complex and multi-dimensional conflicts does not solely rely on elite bargaining, but requires constructive interactions with multiple conflict stakeholders and affected constituencies. This approach also emphasises the roles of, and relations with, a wide range of social actors in the countries of intervention beyond the central state level, including civil society organisations, women, youths, religious actors, and minority groups (e.g. regional, cultural, religious, linguistic or ethnic communities) that have been historically excluded or marginalised by incumbent socio-political elites.

As evidenced in the literature on peace processes and political settlements,[2] there is as yet little consensus among scholars as well as policy-makers on what the concept of inclusivity really entails, who should be included in peace(building) processes, at which stages, on what grounds, and for what (normative or pragmatic) purposes. One of the main dilemmas surrounding this concept pertains to the inclusivity versus effectiveness trade-off, as it is often assumed by conflict parties and mediators alike that highly participatory peace processes might impede the efficiency of decision-making if too many actors and interests are represented at the negotiation table. The purpose of this paper is to assess how EU actors seek to overcome this dilemma when promoting, supporting or facilitating mediation and dialogue processes in third countries, and how local actors assess such interventions. The paper addresses these issues by analysing EU action through a multi-track intervention lens, which assumes that complementary mediation/dialogue channels along various multiple levels of engagement (from elite bargains to grassroots initiatives) might contribute to more effective inclusive peace(building) processes.

The empirical findings are primarily drawn from two case study reports produced in the context of an EU-funded project on Whole-of-Society Conflict Prevention and Peacebuilding (WOSCAP) in Georgia and Yemen, which are based on extensive in-country interviews.[3] Additional secondary literature is used to back up these sources, in addition to primary data gathered through interviews with (current or former) staff

[2]Katia Papagianni, 'Political Transitions after Peace Agreements: The Importance of Consultative and Inclusive Political Processes', *Journal of Intervention and Statebuilding* 3, no.1 (2009), 47–63; Bruce Jones, Molly Elgin-Cossart and Jane Esberg, *Pathways out of fragility: The Case for a Research Agenda on Inclusive Political Settlements in Fragile States* (New York: CIC, 2012); Alina Rocha Menocal, *Inclusive Political Settlements: Evidence, Gaps, and Challenges of Institutional Transformation* (Birmingham, UK: International Development Department, University of Birmingham, 2015); Erwin van Veen and Véronique Dudouet, *Hitting the target, but missing the point? Assessing donor support for inclusive and legitimate politics in fragile societies* (Paris: OECD-DAC, 2017); Jan Pospisil and Alina Rocha Menocal, 'Why political settlements matter: Navigating inclusion in processes of institutional transformation', *Journal of International Development*, Vol 29 (2017), 551–558.

[3]Nana Macharashvili, Ekaterine Basilaia and Nikoloz Samkharade, 'Assessing the EU's conflict prevention and peacebuilding interventions in Georgia', *WOSCAP project deliverable* (2017); Alia Eshaq and Suad al-Marani, 'Assessing the EU's conflict prevention and peacebuilding interventions in Yemen,' *WOSCAP project deliverable* (2017). Both reports can be accessed on the project website: www.woscap.eu.

members of the European External Action Service (EEAS), both in Brussels and in EU Delegations in-country.

The paper is organised as follows: Section 1 provides a brief overview of the growing emphasis on inclusive approaches to peace(building) support by international organisations, including the European Union. Section 2 explores the academic literature on peace processes and political settlements, pertaining to the challenges of designing and implementing inclusive yet effective negotiation or dialogue formats. Section 3 examines how the inclusiveness/effectiveness dilemma plays out empirically in two distinct contexts of EU peacebuilding intervention, namely Georgia and Yemen. Finally the conclusion draws on a comparative analysis of the case study findings to reflect on the merits of a WOS approach to peacebuilding intervention.

Inclusivity: the new normative imperative for mediation and dialogue support

A new global policy consensus seems to have emerged around the promotion of inclusive political settlements. Indeed, the last decade has seen a growing discursive convergence among 'liberal' peacebuilding agencies (at the interface between development, conflict prevention, peace mediation and post-war democratisation) with regards to the assumed benefits of inclusive transition processes from conflict and fragility to peace and resilience. The realisation that the social, economic or political exclusion of large segments of society is a key driver of intra-state wars (as evidenced for instance in the 2011 World Development Report) has prompted donor agencies, diplomats and international organisations, as well as the respective academic communities, to search for the right formula to support inclusive and participatory peacebuilding mechanisms.

The concept of inclusivity is a central pillar of the three major UN review processes conducted in 2015, while the UN Agenda 2030 for Sustainable Development recognises the direct link between inclusivity and peace by calling for all UN member states to promote and support 'inclusive and peaceful societies' (SDG 16).[4] The European Union is progressively – albeit slowly – aligning its own internal policy framework with the global peacebuilding agenda when it comes to the promotion of inclusive engagement in partner countries (i.e. beyond state officials). This shift can be observed by comparing the wording of the EU Comprehensive Approach designed in 2013 with the framing of the 2016 EU Global Strategy. While the former placed its primary focus on EU internal coherence and inter-agency cooperation and barely mentioned the role of non-state actors in the recipient countries,[5] the latter reflects a conscious attempt to address the complexity of conflict-affected societies by acknowledging the range of actors beyond the state and the dynamic relationships that link them. It highlights for instance the EU's ambition to adopt a 'multi-lateral approach engaging all those players present in a conflict and necessary for its resolution',[6] including non-state actors such as the

[4]See https://sustainabledevelopment.un.org/post2015/transformingourworld.

[5]In the EU Commission's Communication on the Comprehensive Approach, civil society is mentioned once in 12 pages, as one actor to engage with in the future, among others such as major international NGOs, think-tanks, academia and public and private actors. See European Commission, *Joint Communication to the European Parliament and the Council – The EU's comprehensive approach to external conflicts and crises* (Brussels: December 2013), 9.

[6]European External Action Service (EEAS), *Shared Vision, Common Action: A Stronger Europe. A Global Strategy for the European Union's Foreign and Security Policy* (June 2016), 29. See online at: http://europa.eu/globalstrategy/en.

private sector and civil society. One can thus argue that the EU global policy agenda is moving closer to a Whole-of-Society approach to peacebuilding intervention in conflict-affected countries by acknowledging the need for multi-level interaction within the recipient societies.

Within the range of EU conflict prevention and peacebuilding instruments and policies (from early warning to crisis management and post-war recovery), this paper is primarily concerned with a comparative assessment of EU ambitions and performance with regards to mediation and dialogue support interventions, as defined by the Concept on Strengthening EU Mediation and Dialogue Capacities (thereafter: EU Concept) endorsed by the EU Council in 2009.[7] Mediation and dialogue support represent key policy domains of EU 'soft power' intervention, which are promoted on both normative and pragmatic grounds. As will be argued later however, the normative values promoted in external engagement might sometimes clash with pragmatic considerations, especially when it comes to the perceived dilemma between inclusive and effective decision-making processes.

Mediation is defined in the EU Concept as 'a way of assisting negotiations between conflict parties and transforming conflicts with the support of an acceptable third party. The general goal of mediation is to enable parties in conflict to reach agreements they find satisfactory and are willing to implement. … Mediation is usually based on a formal mandate from the parties to a conflict, and the mediator gets involved both in the process and substance of the negotiations by making suggestions and proposals'.[8] For its part, dialogue is described in the EU Concept as a less directive approach than mediation, in accordance with the academic literature on third-party conflict intervention.[9] It is defined as 'an open-ended process which aims primarily at creating a culture of communication and search for common ground, leading to confidence building and improved interpersonal understanding among representatives of opposing parties which, in turn, can help to prevent conflict and be a means in reconciliation and peacebuilding processes.'[10] Anchored in social-psychological approaches to peacemaking, dialogue underpins the belief that conflict is not an inter-state or intergovernmental phenomenon but an inter-societal one.[11] The main types of EU intervention in support to mediation and dialogue are described in the EU Concept as: (1) EU officials acting as a (co-)mediator or dialogue facilitator; (2) promoting dialogue and mediation as a non-coercive response to tensions and conflict; (3) leveraging mediation and dialogue through diplomatic and/or economic credence; (4) supporting mediation and dialogue through capacity building, training, logistical support and the provision of expertise to mediators and conflict parties; and (5) funding formal, informal and grassroots mediation and dialogue processes.[12] This diversification of support options beyond direct mediation at the table reflects the complex nature of

[7]Although released nearly a decade ago, the EU Concept has not been revised yet, and thus still represents the main policy guideline for EU staff engaged in mediation and dialogue support activities in third countries (as confirmed by EEAS staff interviewed in March 2017).

[8]Council of the EU, Strengthening EU mediation and dialogue capacities, 2–3.

[9]Amanda E. Feller and Kelly K. Ryan, 'Definition, Necessity, and Nansen: Efficacy of Dialogue in Peacebuilding', *Conflict Resolution Quarterly* 29, no. 5 (2012).

[10]Council of the EU, *Strengthening EU mediation and dialogue capacities*, 3.

[11]Herbert C. Kelman, 'Interactive problem solving: Changing political culture in the pursuit of conflict resolution', *Peace and Conflict: Journal of Peace Psychology* 16, no. 4 (2010), 389–413.

[12]Council of the EU, Strengthening EU mediation and dialogue capacities, 8.

contemporary peace support architectures, which are becoming more sophisticated, involving multi-stakeholder mediation teams combined with strong local ownership mechanisms.[13]

These EU policy guidelines are strongly anchored in an inclusive approach to mediation, defined by the UN Guidance Note for Effective Mediation as 'the extent and manner in which the views and needs of conflict parties and other stakeholders are represented and integrated into the process and outcome of a mediation effort'.[14] Indeed, the EU Concept recognises the need to 'be involved in mediation processes at various levels – from the governmental to that of local communities' and to pursue 'a top-down and a bottom-up approach in parallel tracks, which reinforce and inform each other'.[15] It also argues that thanks to the EU's 'engagement at the grassroots level and its emphasis on civil society development, this holistic approach on conflict resolution contributes to the development of a unique and differentiated role for the EU amongst other providers of international peace mediation'.[16] The EU Concept also includes the promotion of women's participation as a guiding principle, in reference to UN Security Council Resolutions 1325 and 1820 on women, peace and security. However, there is no explicit reference to other social groups such as youth, ethnic/religious minorities, traditional authorities or local religious elites.

In essence, the EU understands inclusivity in the context of mediation and dialogue support as a multi-track approach combining top-down and bottom-up intervention, with a particular emphasis on strengthening the participation or representation of specific segments of civil society (such as women), while other societal actors have been largely disregarded so far.

Inclusive and effective peace processes: a contradiction in terms?

While the quest for inclusive peace processes has been at the forefront of the international agenda in the past few years, there is still a lot of confusion within both the scholarly and practitioner communities when it comes to defining inclusivity and applying its principles to complex cases of protracted intra-state conflicts characterised by a constellation of parties and interests. The dictionary definition of inclusivity (or inclusiveness) refers to 'the fact or policy of not excluding members or participants on the grounds of gender, race, class, sexuality, disability, etc'.[17] In the context of political settlements, policy analysts define inclusive political transitions as 'two-level games' that comprise both inter-elite interactions between incumbent and emerging power-holders, and broader linkages between the state and society.[18] With regards to the first dimension, the concept of 'inclusive enough' coalitions introduced by the 2011 World Development Report invokes the need for post-war transitions to involve all key

[13]Stine Lehmann-Larsen, 'Effectively supporting mediation: Developments, challenges and requirements', *Oslo Forum Papers*, no. 3 (Geneva: Centre for Humanitarian Dialogue, 2014).
[14]United Nations (UN), *Guidance for Effective Mediation* (2012), 11. See online at: www.un.org/wcm/webdav/site/undpa/shared/undpa/pdf/UN%20Guidance%20for%20Effective%20Mediation.pdf.
[15]Council of the EU, *Strengthening EU mediation and dialogue capacities*, 7.
[16]Ibid.
[17]See www.collinsdictionary.com/dictionary/english/inclusivity.
[18]Asia Foundation, 'Political Settlements: Implications for International Development Policy and Practice', *Occasional Paper* 2 (July 2010); OECD-DAC, 'From Power Struggle to Sustainable Peace: Understanding Political Settlements', *Conflict and Stability Series* (OECD Publishing, 2011); Pospisil and Rocha Menocal, 'Why political settlements matter'.

stakeholders who have the capacity to implement and/or spoil peace and who represent important constituencies.[19] This includes formal and informal actors who have significant economic, social, cultural, political and/or military leverage – ranging from governments, army leaders and political opposition groups (armed and unarmed), to business elites or large landowners as well as religious and traditional authorities.[20] When it comes to the state-society level, inclusivity is rather defined as the extent to which larger segments of the population have access to, and influence over, decision making – with a specific emphasis on (previously) marginalised societal sectors who by tradition, culture or history have limited resources and entry points to access, influence and participate in the power infrastructure.[21]

The rationale put forward in the peacebuilding and development literature for promoting inclusive political settlements lies in the assumed benefits of participatory decision-making processes on the resulting outcomes, especially with regards to their legitimacy (i.e. societal acceptance and support) and sustainability.[22] For instance, some studies have demonstrated the positive effects of civil society or women's participation for the durability of peaceful settlements.[23] Yet, in spite of this recent surge in policy and academic interest in the subject-matter of inclusivity, we still know little about how much inclusivity is 'inclusive enough' for efficient decision-making. Many peace processes that were designed in a highly participatory fashion (such as in Guatemala) failed to be effectively implemented, and thus one cannot take for granted that inclusivity necessarily leads to better results in terms of bringing about a more representative and responsive governance system.[24] Indeed, one of the most acute dilemmas in this field pertains to the challenges of designing and implementing inclusive, yet effective peace processes. Although inclusivity is often connoted with effectiveness,[25] this relationship is also a matter of debate and raises a few challenges. For instance, the multiplication of actors with divergent interests at the negotiation table may make a settlement harder to reach and lead to an unworkable compromise.[26] Similarly, the drive towards inclusiveness and broad representation through extensive power-sharing provisions might be detrimental for state coherence and effectiveness – it can lead to such a dispersion of

---

[19]World Bank, *World Development Report 2011. Conflict, Security and Development* (2011).

[20]Asia Foundation, 'Political Settlements'.

[21]Véronique Dudouet and Stina Lundström, 'Post-war Political Settlements: From Participatory Transition Processes to Inclusive State-building and Governance', *Berghof Research Report* (Berlin: Berghof Foundation, 2016).

[22]Papagianni, 'Political Transitions after Peace Agreements; Jones et al., *Pathways out of Fragility*; Charles Call, *Why Peace Fails: The Causes and Prevention of Civil War* (Washington, DC: Georgetown, 2012); Franzisca Zanker, 'Legitimate Representation: Civil Society Actors in Peace Negotiations Revisited', *International Negotiation*, no.19 (2014): 62–88; Seth Kaplan and Mark Freeman, *Inclusive Transitions Framework* (Barcelona: Institute for Inclusive Transitions, 2015).

[23]Anthony Wanis – St. John and Darren Kew, 'Civil Society and Peace Negotiations: Confronting Exclusion', *International Negotiation*, Vol. 13 (2008): 11–36; Christine Bell, 'Women and peace processes, negotiations, and agreements: operational opportunities and challenges', *NOREF Policy Brief* (2013); Desirée Nilsson, 'Anchoring the Peace: Civil Society Actors in Peace Accords and Durable Peace', *International Interactions*, Vol.38, Issue 2 (2012);

Thania Paffenholz, 'Can Inclusive Peace Processes Work? New Evidence From a Multi-Year Research Project', *Policy Brief* (Geneva: Centre on Conflict, Development, Graduate Institute of International and Development Studies, 2015); Thania Paffenholz, Nick Ross, Steven Dixon, Anna-Lena Schluchter and Jacqui True, *Making Women Count – Not Just Counting Women: assessing Women's Inclusion and Influence on Peace Negotiations* (Geneva: Inclusive Peace and Security Transition Initiative, 2016).

[24]Dudouet and Lundström, 'Post-war Political Settlements'; Castillejo, 'Dilemmas and experiences'.

[25]Rocha Menocal, *Inclusive Political Settlements*; Department for International Development (DFID) *Building Peaceful States and Societies: A DFID Practice Paper* (2010); Mushtaq H. Khan, *Political Settlements and the Governance of Growth-Enhancing Institutions* (SOAS eprints, 2010). See online at: http://eprints.soas.ac.uk/9968/1/Political_Settlements_internet.pdf.

[26]OECD-DAC, 'From Power Struggle to Sustainable Peace', 31–32.

power and authority that a political system becomes paralysed and unable to carry out critical governance reforms.[27]

Effective inclusion within peacemaking arenas is also conditioned by the ability of participants to influence the decision-making process and outcomes. Indeed, negotiation tables or national dialogue formats are often inherently characterised by power asymmetries, since participants tend to have unequal levels of (technical, structural, cultural) capacities, power and resources. It can be argued that the 'internal exclusion'[28] of non-elites, when their participation is not accompanied by effective decision-making power or influence, brings with it the risk of turning such constituencies into 'spoilers', as – as argued by a South Sudanese researcher – 'a superficial invitation to the table without genuine inclusion of their demands will also cause them to have superficial commitment to peace'.[29] A recent study of 40 political transition processes by the Graduate Institute of International Development Studies found that only if societal actors are 'meaningfully' included, agreements are more likely to be reached and sustained.[30]

This inclusivity/effectiveness dilemma underlines the necessity for mediators such as the EU to support the design of 'inclusive enough' deliberation processes that enable a genuine participatory process without impeding the efficiency of decision-making. In the remainder of this section, we briefly present three approaches to 'inclusive enough' political settlements proposed by peacebuilding experts in order to solve this dilemma, which will be subsequently empirically tested through the prism of EU mediation and dialogue support in Georgia and Yemen.

Option 1: inclusive dialogue formats with deadlock-breaking mechanisms

Inclusive decision-making formats designed to codify new political settlements during democratic transitions or peace processes often take the form of national dialogues, which aim to involve a wide number of direct participants beyond ruling elite and primary opposition groups, and usually provide guarantees for minority participation (e.g. through quotas or allocated seats for non-elite representatives). In order to prevent such inclusive settings from impeding the efficiency of decision-making, many national dialogues provide for deadlock-breaking mechanisms such as consensus-building commissions or informal taskforces.[31]

Option 2: capacity-building for marginalised groups at the bargaining table

External third-parties involved in mediation and dialogue support often seek to bridge the gap between inclusive participation and effective decision-making by providing technical or diplomatic support to participants in order to enhance their chances of

---

[27]Alina Rocha Menocal, 'State Building for Peace : a new Paradigm for International Engagement in Post-Conflict Fragile States?', *Third World Quarterly* 32, no.10 (2011), 37–41.

[28]Angela M. Banks, 'Expanding Participation in Constitution Making: Challenges and Opportunities', *William and Mary Law Review*, 48 (2008), 1043–1069.

[29]Jok Madut Jok, 'The Paradox of Peace in Sudan and South Sudan. Why the Political Settlements Failed to Endure', *Inclusive Political Settlements* No. 15 (Berlin: Berghof Foundation, 2015), 7.

[30]Paffenholz, 'Can Inclusive Peace Processes Work?'

[31]Berghof Foundation, National Dialogue Handbook: A Guide for Practitioners (Berlin: Berghof Foundation, 2017).

'meaningful inclusion', and empowering disadvantaged groups, such as opposition parties, civil society actors or even armed movements, to participate effectively in negotiations.[32]

Options 3: multi-track consultation or coordination channels

The multi-track model of diplomacy acknowledges that peace processes do not only rely on elite-led bargaining deals, but also need to operate at multiple entry-points within a conflict-affected society, from top-level decision-makers to grassroots communities.[33] *Track 1* refers to official discussions between high-level governmental and military leaders focusing on ceasefires, peace talks, treaties and other agreements. Often associated with power-based, deal-brokering diplomacy by external 'mediators with muscles', Track 1 negotiations are typically limited to a small number of national stakeholders, while other segments of society tend to be excluded from such processes.

Track 2 (or Track 1,5) refers to unofficial dialogue and problem-solving activities aimed at building relationships between civil society leaders and influential individuals who have the ability to impact the official level dynamics through lobbying, advocacy or consultation channels. Indeed, one of the most common methods of broadening participation beyond the primary contenders during negotiation processes consists of setting up parallel informal dialogue or consultation channels for influencing elitist decision-making formats from the outside. Such mechanisms are frequently supported by international agencies, but they tend to lack binding feedback loops and monitoring mechanisms to ensure that issues and concerns raised by the participants would be effectively transferred to the negotiation table and integrated in their codified outcomes.[34]

Finally, *Track 3* diplomacy refers to inter- or intra-community dialogue activities at the grassroots level to encourage mutual interaction and understanding. This track highlights international actors' need to engage with and support actors who are typically overlooked by the other diplomatic tracks, who make up the fabric of society and who are deeply affected by violent conflict. Grassroots 'people-to-people' dialogue projects are often funded by international donors such as the EU, through dedicated instruments such as the Instrument contributing to Stability and Peace (IcSP) or the European Instrument for Democracy and Human Rights (EIDHR). The biggest challenge however is to introduce feedback loop mechanisms to ensure that these efforts are coordinated with Track 1 and 2 mechanisms, so that grassroots engagement may contribute to 'peace writ large'[35] and that top-level intervention 'trickles down' across society.

---

[32] Véronique Dudouet, 'Mediating Peace with Proscribed Armed Groups,' *USIP Special Report*, 2010, see online at: www.usip.org/sites/default/files/SR239Duduoet.pdf.

[33] Louise Diamond and John McDonald, *Multi-Track Diplomacy: A Systems Approach to Peace*. Second Edition (Washington, DC: Institute for Multi-Track Diplomacy, 1993); John Paul Lederach, *Building Peace: Sustainable Reconciliation in Divided Societies* (Washington, D.C.: United States Institute of Peace, 1997).

[34] Dudouet and Lundström, 'Post-War Political Settlements'.

[35] Collaborative for Development Action (CDA), *Reflecting on Peace Practice Handbook* (Cambridge, MA: CDA Collaborative Learning Projects, 2004).

In sum, one basic implication of the multi-track approach is that not all societal voices necessarily need to be directly represented at Track 1, but information-sharing ought to flow towards/from other tracks of dialogue engagement.

Assessing EU multi-track mediation and dialogue support in Georgia and Yemen

The purpose of this section is to examine empirically to what extent, and by which means, the European Union as an international peacebuilding agency seeks to support avenues to address the 'inclusivity/effectiveness' dilemma during political settlements, by influencing the design, contents and outcome of negotiation arenas; by bringing excluded stakeholders ('hard to reach' actors, marginalised groups, civil society) to the negotiation table itself and supporting their capacity for meaningful participation; and/or by linking Track 1 processes with parallel Track 2 dialogue arenas and Track 3 inter-community dialogue initiatives.

The empirical data is drawn from two case studies: Georgia and Yemen.[36] These two countries represent contrasting cases of EU peacebuilding intervention with regards to their geographic and political proximity to the EU (within the European neighbourhood and beyond); the main purpose of negotiations (to build confidence between the parties in Georgia, or to transform the state in Yemen); and the main Track 1 negotiation formats supported by the international community (from a classical closed-door elite bargain strategy in Georgia to a highly inclusive national dialogue in Yemen). Despite dissimilar peace process designs, both countries share a number of similar challenges when it comes to the meaningful inclusion of marginalised groups and 'hard to reach' actors from breakaway regions or so-called 'radical' opposition groups. Both conflicts are also highly influenced by the role of powerful neighbours (e.g. Russia and Saudi Arabia), which in turn has a major impact on the perceptions, influence and strategic considerations of external parties such as the EU. Finally, the wide range of EU actors and instruments involved in multi-track conflict resolution efforts in both countries (through direct intervention or in support to other international actors) enables us to analyse the whole spectrum of mediation and dialogue support activities defined in Section 1 and the range of approaches introduced in Section 2 to address the inclusivity/effectiveness dilemma.

Georgia

The conflict in Georgia represents a prominent case of direct involvement by EU diplomats in high-level mediation of a territorial dispute in the European neighbourhood. EU mediation in Georgia has so far been unable to leverage sufficient power to induce the conflict parties – including Russia – to conclude any significant agreement on the resolution of the protracted conflict in the South Caucasus. The Six-point Peace Plan that ended the five-day armed conflict over the status of breakaway regions South-Ossetia and Abkhazia in August 2008 was mediated by the French President Sarkozy

[36]These cases were investigated as part of the WOSCAP project on EU civilian peacebuilding and conflict prevention capabilities (www.woscap.eu).

while France held the EU Presidency. However, the implementation of this plan has proven difficult and the conflict is considered as 'frozen', while Russia has become more deeply entrenched in the separatist regions.

The role of the EU in Track 1 mediation and dialogue efforts is mainly concerned with the Geneva International Discussions (GID), which were launched in October 2008 to address the consequences of the Georgia-Russia war and Russia's subsequent recognition of the independence of Abkhazia and South Ossetia. For eight years, this format has been the only platform to discuss conflict-related humanitarian and security issues, and can also be assessed as acting as a preventive diplomacy instrument to pre-empt any further re-escalation of the conflict. The EU is currently co-chairing the mediated GID with the Organisation for Security and Co-operation in Europe (OSCE) and the UN. The Geneva process brings together representatives from Georgia, the Russian Federation, the United States and Georgia's breakaway regions. All participants attend the GID in their personal capacities rather than as official delegations. The EU is primarily represented by the EU Special Representative for the South Caucasus and the Crisis in Georgia (EUSR), who is mandated to 'contribute to a peaceful settlement of conflicts in the region'.[37] Georgian civil society interviewees consider the GID as an exclusionary and elitist process taking place behind closed doors, especially given the lack of civil society involvement (from all sides of the conflict), which prevents them from either participating in, or monitoring, the talks. No information is available on the issues presented during the meetings, the points made by different participants and the results of the talks.[38] Moreover, the GID is dominated by men (due to the composition of the state organs participating in the process) and pays little attention to gender aspects.[39]

At the Track 2 (or Track 1,5) level of engagement, EU Special Representatives in the Caucasus have played a key dialogue facilitation role by 'providing a direct communication channel ... with actors with whom the EU cannot deal through official channels'.[40] In Georgia, the EUSR combines a representation role within the GID with a mandate to engage in confidence-building activities with civil society actors in the whole region. He and his team regularly consult local civil society actors in Abkhazia, and draw on their information and analysis. According to these officials, there have been several attempts to make the views expressed by civil society actors heard by participants in the formal political and security dialogue process. Debriefings after each GID rounds have been held for Georgian civil society organisations (CSOs) and international experts, which also allowed for collecting their own proposals on how to move the negotiation process forward. Also, parallel meetings between Georgian officials and Abkhaz CSOs have taken place, and addressed many issues relevant to the formal negotiation process. In addition, efforts have been made to organise 'technical' problem-solving workshops, both in the margins and outside of the GID rounds, which involved experts and professionals from different sides to address practical issues faced

---

[37]Council of the EU, *New EU Special Representative for the South Caucasus and the crisis in Georgia appointed* (8 July 2014), see online at: www.consilium.europa.eu/uedocs/cms_data/docs/pressdata/EN/foraff/143711.pdf.

[38]Macharashvili et al., 'Assessing the EU's conflict prevention', 32.

[39]Ibid., 44.

[40]MediatEUr, *Debriefing EU Mediators: Summary and key lessons from a debriefing with former EUSR for the South Caucasus, Peter Semneby* (Brussels: MediatEUr, 2012), 3.

by conflict-affected communities (such as cultural archives and environmental threats), which are seen as less controversial than those being dealt with in the formal negotiations.[41] Another EU institution, the EU Monitoring Mission in Georgia (EUMM) is also involved in Track 2 confidence-building measures by maintaining continuous working relationships with government officials and civil society representatives, and thus has the potential to support multi-track mediation efforts.[42]

Finally, the EU is a major funder of Track 3 grassroots dialogue initiatives. The IcSP has been funding since 2010 a Confidence Building Early Response Mechanism (COBERM) implemented by the United Nations Development Programme (UNDP), aiming to 'stimulate people-to-people contacts across conflict divides, and to generate increased capacities within communities as well as CSOs to mediate political differences in constructive ways'.[43] COBERM has been the only mechanism to successfully engage with civil society actors (such as journalists, academics and researchers) across de facto Georgian divisions, both at the intra- and inter-community level.[44]

The main challenges related to Track 2 and 3 dialogue facilitation, when it comes to the inclusivity/efficiency dilemma, are concerned with civil society capacity-building, the inclusion of 'hard to reach' constituencies, and multi-track coordination. Strengthening local CSOs under the COBERM scheme aims to benefit Abkhazian and South Ossetian societies equally, but the latter are hardly able to access the funds due to the underdeveloped level of civil society in that territory. Moreover, given the complex and work-intensive EU application procedures and accounting regulations, only a limited group of local organisations have the necessary capabilities to apply for the COBERM programme.[45]

The second challenge pertains to the EU's access to actors and institutions in the breakaway regions, to support their inclusion in multi-track mediation and dialogue efforts. Russian authorities are restricting the freedom of movement within Abkhazia and South Ossetia, which impedes the ability of local CSOs to cooperate with international actors and to participate in dialogue activities, and in turn, restricts access to these territories. Individuals from the breakaway regions face safety risks when participating in Track 2 and 3 dialogue activities. Moreover, EU efforts to support cross-community confidence-building are constrained by the lack of trust in the EU as an impartial broker among inhabitants of the contested territories. Indeed, while the EU tries to position itself as a non-partisan third-party, its commitment to Georgian territorial integrity and long-standing policy of 'engagement without recognition' with the de-facto authorities of Abkhazia and South Ossetia have fuelled perceptions of EU bias by these stakeholders.[46]

---

[41]Interview with EUSR political advisor in Brussels, March 2017.

[42]Catriona Gourlay, *Mediation and Dialogue as Tools for EU CSDP Missions* (Initiative for Peacebuilding, 2010); Andrew Sherriff, Volker Hauck and Camilla Rocca, 'Glass half full: Study on EU lessons learnt in mediation and dialogue', Study submitted to the European External Action Service by ECDPM through the AETS Consortium – Cardno (Maastricht: ECDPM, 2013).

[43]Macharashvili et al., 'Assessing the EU's conflict prevention', 35.

[44]United Nations Development Programme (UNDP), *Final Evaluation report on COBERM* (2012). See online at: http://erc.undp.org/evaluation/documents/downloadad/6141.

[45]Macharashvili et al., 'Assessing the EU's conflict prevention', 40–41.

[46]Macharashvili et al., 'Assessing the EU's conflict prevention', 34; Magdalena Frichova Grono, *Georgia's conflicts: What role for the EU as mediator?* (International Alert/Initiative for Peacebuilding, March 2010).

The final key challenge is concerned with the lack of cross-track coordination and synergies. Efforts to enable conflict actors to engage informally on concrete everyday concerns remain disconnected from the official negotiation arena and have very limited influence (if any at all) on the GID. EU support for grassroots-level dialogue and reconciliation work also seems to be insufficiently connected to the other tracks of engagement, which reduces their bottom-up effectiveness and impact. Suitable interlocutors that can systematically and purposefully coordinate the different actors involved across multiple levels of engagement are rare. The involvement of high-level EU officials in the COBERM project in Georgia represents a welcome exception: the EU Head of Delegation is a member of its steering group, which 'is a very unusual arrangement, because very rarely such kind of high-level officials will be involved in programming' of EU-funded Track II and III activities.[47] However, despite such high-level involvement, no direct transfer of learning and knowledge between COBERM projects and the GID has been recorded so far.

Yemen

Yemen represents a contrasting case of EU involvement outside its geographic neighbourhood, where the EU has not played any leading mediating role but has rather supported an internally-led dialogue process in coordination with other multinational actors, through joint diplomatic initiatives or complementary diplomatic, outreach and capacity-building activities. The EU was a party to the 'Group of Friends of Yemen' (FoY) group established in January 2010, to address the multiple causes of instability in Yemen such as the activities of Al-Qaida in the Arabian Peninsula, and internal conflicts with Yemeni state challengers such as the Houthi opposition movement and South-based protestors demanding self-determination.[48] When popular protests awakened by the so-called Arab Spring threatened to escalate the conflict in 2011, UK and US Ambassadors together with the EU Head of Delegation initiated international discussions that led to an agreement on a peaceful transition process in Yemen with the Gulf Cooperation Council (GCC). The 'Agreement on the implementation mechanism for the transition process in Yemen', also called GCC Agreement, brokered with President Saleh in November 2011 aimed for a two-year transition process culminating in a national dialogue and a new Constitution.

The EU's role during the National Dialogue Conference (NDC) will be used here to illustrate the approaches to 'inclusive enough' political settlements introduced in Section 2. The NDC, held in Sana'a from 18 March 2013 to 24 January 2014, was designed to set the foundations for a new constitution. Following the transition of power from former President Saleh to his deputy, current President Hadi, a technical committee composed of a wide range of stakeholders was mandated to design the NDC bylaw. The technical committee set the criteria for participation in the NDC, such as the inclusion of women, youth, and representatives from the Houthis and Southern separatist movements. The NDC involved 565 delegates, organised into 11 political groups, in addition to 20 minor political parties. It also had representative quotas of 30% for

[47]Macharashvili et al., 'Assessing the EU's conflict prevention', 37.
[48]Eshaq and al-Marani, 'Assessing the EU's conflict prevention and peacebuilding'.

women, 20% for youth, and 50% for southerners, for the NDC overall as well as within each political group's delegation.

The EU played a prominent role in supporting an inclusive decision-making process during the NDC, especially through public diplomacy. One component of the EU strategy in Yemen since 2011 has been the promotion of marginalised constituencies and excluded actors in the peaceful transition process. For instance, the EU Council issued a declaration urging all Yemeni stakeholders to ensure that the national dialogue would be 'fully inclusive, balanced, and transparent, adequately representing all strands of the Yemeni society and reflecting the important role of youth and women'.[49] Besides diplomatic advocacy, one major task of the EU Delegation ahead of the NDC was to conduct outreach to those groups that had not been included in the negotiations of the GCC Initiative. By bringing the Houthis, CSOs, the moderate wing of al-Hiraak and representatives of the youth and women to the table, the EU Delegation officials tried to pave the way for an inclusive process.[50] During the NDC itself, the EU sought to conduct specific outreach activities towards non-elite participants, with special attention to youth and women's organisations, to support their active inclusion and to encourage them to adopt a common negotiation position.

Beyond the formal setting of the NDC, the EU Delegation in Sana'a played a pivotal role in facilitating Track 2 inter-party dialogue between the various parties, by offering an informal neutral space where stakeholders could meet and explore their respective positions and interests in a confidential atmosphere.[51] Despite the official EU standpoint of support to territorial integrity and national unity, this pro-state bias has not affected its perceived impartiality, as the EUD was able to host discussions and maintain regular contact with two prominent state challengers, the Houthis and the Southern movement, to try and address their grievances in the transitional period. After the conclusion of the NDC, these channels of communication were maintained, despite the Saudi-led military intervention initiated in 2015. The EUD conducted low-key diplomacy in trying to reach out to some of the conflict parties, most importantly the Houthis, building upon dialogue channels that had been established during the NDC.[52]

With regards to Track 2 and 3 engagement with sub-national and civil society actors, the EU sponsored a series of local dialogues at the governorate level to support the political participation of Yemeni citizens and the main stakeholders (e.g. political parties, women, youth, civil society and businesses), in parallel to the NDC. These activities were carried out by the Yemeni NGO Political Development Forum and the German Berghof Foundation.[53] The EU has also supported various dialogue platforms for civil society representatives, for example by sponsoring a trust-building conference in Cyprus in October 2015 that brought together Yemeni women from different

[49]Council of the European Union, 'Council Conclusions on Yemen', 3199th Foreign Affairs Council Meeting (Brussels, 19 November 2012). EU High Representative/Vice President Catherine Ashton also made public statements following the launch of the Yemen National Dialogue, and at the occasion of its closing session. See http://eu-un.europa.eu/statement-by-eu-hr-ashton-following-the-launch-of-the-yemen-national-dialogue/; and http://eu-un.europa.eu/statement-by-eu-hr-ashton-on-the-closing-of-yemens-national-dialogue-conference/.

[50]Natalie Girke, 'A matter of balance: the European Union as a mediator in Yemen,' *European Security* 24, no.4 (2015), 509–524.

[51]Ibid.

[52]Eshaq and al-Marani, 'Assessing the EU's conflict prevention and peacebuilding', 31.

[53]See online at: www.pdf-yemen.com/index.php/en/our-program/current-projects/strengthening-public-participation-local-dialogues.

political and social backgrounds.[54] Finally, the IcSP is currently supporting two grassroots inter-community projects, one carried out by the NGO Search for Common Ground to support local dialogues on reconciliation, inter- or intra-faith issues, and resources-based conflicts; and the other one implemented by Saferworld on capacity-building for women activists and CSOs to engage in local peacebuilding processes.[55]

Despite the proactive engagement of EU staff in Brussels and in-country to support inclusive multi-track dialogue channels from the top-level NDC down to grassroots projects, the on-going war raging in Yemen is a tragic reminder of the ultimate failure of the peace and transition process initiated through the 2011 GCC agreement. All three approaches to resolving the inclusivity/effectiveness dilemma highlighted in Section 2 were applied in Yemen, but they faced some serious challenges, which have prevented successful mediation and dialogue efforts so far.

First, strategies aimed at improving the capacity of minority groups and marginalised social actors to participate effectively in the NDC were hampered by these actors' failures to mobilise around common positions. For instance, even though southerners represented 50% of NDC delegates, they were fractured by internal polarisations on the question of federalism, and their inability to adopt a common stance made it harder to identify a mutually acceptable compromise – which suggests that a south-south dialogue should have preceded the north-south dialogue during the NDC.[56] The women delegates also failed to translate their participation into effective influence, partly due to the discriminatory norms and attitudes towards women which prevail in Yemeni society, including within the NDC.[57] Some interviewed Yemeni stakeholders criticised the selection mechanisms for civil society participants, asserting that the NDC was still dominated by the old political establishment with no real outreach to other components of society.[58] Secondly, the introduction of deadlock-breaking mechanisms to speed up the process of decision-making in the NDC was assessed as quite ambivalent. On the one hand, the sub-division of the NDC into nine working groups facilitated the process of consensus-building by smaller groups of delegates, allowing them to reach the required 90% majority vote on most issues. On the other hand, the excessive powers allocated to a central 'consensus committee' in charge of solving the most controversial issues had a negative impact on the inclusivity of the decision-making process, which was progressively removed from the large conference and delegated to a small group of delegates handpicked by President Hadi.[59]

When it comes to the EU's ability to engage with 'difficult actors' such as state challengers, the channels of communication established during the NDC and maintained during the early phase of the war became seriously affected by the lack of EU presence on the ground after the evacuation of all Delegation and member state Embassies' staff. The EU's perceived neutrality on the ground was also impeded by the proactive role of some of its member states (especially the United Kingdom) in

[54]Eshaq and al-Marani, 'Assessing the EU's conflict prevention and peacebuilding', 31.
[55]A description of all IcSP-funded projects can be found online at: https://icspmap.eu/.
[56]Ali Saif Hassan, 'Yemen National Dialogue Conference: managing peaceful change? In Legitimacy and peace processes: from coercion to consent,' *Accord* 25 (London: Conciliation Resources, 2014), 54.
[57]Castillejo, 'Dilemmas and experiences'.
[58]Eshaq and al-Marani, 'Assessing the EU's conflict prevention and peacebuilding', 34–53.
[59]Erica Gaston, 'Process Lessons Learned in Yemen's National Dialogue', *USIP Special Report*, No. 342 (2014), 6.

supporting Saudi Arabia-led airstrikes since 2015, as assessed by some interviewed stakeholders (most prominently Houthi respondents).[60]

Finally, multi-track coordination and synergies also suffered from serious flaws, as the EU did not put sufficient efforts into linking the outcomes of Track 2 dialogue initiatives (sponsored by the European Commission) into the NDC, and failed to support NGOs involved in such processes to leverage these efforts diplomatically. For example, although external outreach and consultation with civil society, the media and the Yemeni public represented an important part of the NDC, these efforts were 'carried out in a shallow way, and the input and feedback gathered were not properly streamed into the deliberations of the NDC'.[61]

Conclusion

The 2009 EU concept represented a bold attempt to raise the profile of EU soft-power diplomacy through mediation and dialogue engagement, and especially highlighted an innovative approach to inclusive multi-track diplomacy. This framework has created significant awareness across EU institutions on the importance of multi-track efforts in conflict-affected countries and a widespread recognition that inclusive and participatory dialogue formats are essential ingredients for effective and sustainable peace processes.[62] However, judging by the evidence from the two cases explored in this paper, there is still a significant gap between the policy expectations for a WOS approach to mediation and dialogue support and the realities on the ground.

A comparative assessment of the negotiation formats adopted in Georgia and Yemen brings to light a significant paradox. Indeed, in a context such as Georgia where the EU is involved directly in Track I mediation and thus would be assumed to have more influence and leverage to support or induce the participation of marginalised groups at the negotiation table, there is no direct involvement of non-state actors beyond the incumbent elites and primary conflict stakeholders. Civil society is only informed and consulted on the mediated negotiations through parallel 'technical' tracks and preparatory/briefing meetings. The focus of EU dialogue support efforts is rather on Track 3 confidence-building and reconciliation efforts across communities affected by the conflict. By contrast, in a context like post-2011 Yemen where the EU was not in the driving seat of the mediation but rather assisted – along with other third-parties – a nationally led process of national dialogue through diplomatic and technical support, this format ended up being far more inclusive and participatory.

Many factors might contribute to this discrepancy, one of them being the role of regional geopolitics. While GCC members and the Group of Friends of Yemen – including the EU – shared common interests in a Yemeni peaceful transition (at least until the 2015 war), Russia represents a powerful counter-power in Georgia, whose interests (such as its firm opposition to any direct civil society participation at the bargaining table) dictate the format of the GID talks and sharply lessen the leverage of the EU as a mediator. As a result, the EU is seen in the region as a mediator 'without

[60] Eshaq and al-Marani, 'Assessing the EU's conflict prevention and peacebuilding'.
[61] Hassan, 'Yemen National Dialogue Conference', 53.
[62] Interviews with three MST staff members (Brussels, EEAS, March 2017).

muscle'.[63] While there may be some opportunities for positive incentives towards Georgia, such as through the 2017 Association Agreement,[64] there is very little the EU could offer South Ossetia, Abkhazia or Russia. Polarised positions among EU member states on what stance to adopt towards Russia also prevent a more proactive approach and result in a sharp contrast between the EU's high level of economic, political and security interests in the region and its lack of actual leverage on the ground.[65]

For its part, the Yemeni case illustrates the challenges of designing inclusive formal negotiation arenas, such as a national dialogue, while ensuring an effective decision-making process and a meaningful influence by all participants on the codified outcome. The experience of women, youth and other non-elite participants in the NDC seems to reflect a common trend among international donors to focus on quantitative over qualitative representation, as the limited political skills and experience of such stakeholders prevented them from translating their nominal inclusion into meaningful influence over decision-making outcomes.[66] Donors' attempts to empower civil society groups by offering technical capacity-building support failed to bridge this gap, given that most crucial decisions were ultimately made by a handful of individuals hand-picked by the President (thus distorting the original goal of deadlock-breaking mechanisms), and as broader societal norms privileging the incumbent socio-political elites remain unchanged. This finding thus suggests that external support for inclusive peace processes should entail complementary strategies aimed at sensitising EU staff and incentivising national elites on the benefits of political as well as social inclusionary norms, while simultaneously empowering marginalised groups to participate effectively in dialogue and decision-making arenas.

Finally, despite the sharp contrast in their negotiation and decision-making formats, the Georgian and Yemeni peace/transition processes present quite similar findings when it comes to the challenges of multi-track coordination. On the positive side, the two case studies seem to indicate that the EU displays the capacity to deploy the full range of multi-track approaches to mediation and dialogue listed in Section 1. Nevertheless, there is a lack of institutional mechanisms and political guidance to strengthen synergies between the various levels of diplomatic or technical intervention, which reduces the potential (and misses the opportunity) to maximise their impact.

The challenges around multi-track coordination in dialogue and mediation illustrate the difficulties to operationalise the integrated multilateral approach to foreign policy put forward by the 2016 EU Global Strategy. Coming back to the WOS approach elaborated in this Special Issue, the inherent challenges related to state-society inclusivity illustrated in this paper point to the added value of combining vertical multi-actor engagement with horizontal inter-sectorial comprehensiveness, as suggested by the WOS framework. In particular, the cases of Georgia and Yemen illustrates that people-centred inclusivity in Track 1 political negotiation processes is not always a realistic option, but might be effectively compensated by coordinated intervention along various

[63]Macharashvili et al., 'Assessing the EU's conflict prevention', 34.

[64]European Union, *Association Agreement between the European Union and the European Atomic Energy Community and their Member States, of the one part, and Georgia, of the other part* (30 August 2014).

[65]Frichova Grono, 'Georgia's conflicts'.

[66]Van Veen and Dudouet, 'Hitting the Target'.

domains of soft power intervention. Concretely, the EU's sources of leverage in a country such as Yemen are rooted in its local perception as a 'credible humanitarian and development actor with a long-term experience of engaging in conflict regions', which is 'critical to its credibility in supporting the more political peace process'.[67] The multiplicity of entry-points for EU institutions to access and interact with local state and civil society stakeholders can only be coordinated effectively, however, if their various policy goals (e.g. stability, development, democracy, human rights) and those of all their member states are aligned – which seems to be hardly the case currently in Georgia and Yemen. For instance, the EU's ambition to promote a more coherent approach to external conflicts and crisis, as portrayed in its Global Strategy, is seriously challenged in Yemen, where some Member States seek to re-prioritise dialogue options while others are actively supporting the Saudi-led hard power military offensive against the Houthis. Therefore, the two axes of the WOS approach helpfully emphasise that attempts to increase the range of (state and non-state) stakeholders involved in peace-(building) processes should not be promoted at the expense of horizontal inter-sectorial coherence and coordination.

Both negotiation formats scrutinised in this paper – the Geneva International Discussions and the National Dialogue Conference – have failed to bring about sustainable 'positive peace' in Georgia and Yemen. The former have not brought any tangible outcomes in the South Caucasus yet, besides preserving the status quo and committing the parties to confront one another peacefully in negotiations rather than through violent means.[68] The latter produced a highly inclusive codified agreement but which never became implemented, as the escalation of inter-party rivalries plunged the country into a devastating civil war. Despite the poor achievements brought about so far by the GID and the NDC, inclusive mediation and dialogue approaches might still be pursued for their inherent normative value, even though their strategic impact in terms of sustainability and legitimacy remains a matter of debate. But for these laudable goals to become a realistic option in political bargaining processes conditioned by strategic and geopolitical priorities, there is still a long way to go.

Disclosure statement

No potential conflict of interest was reported by the authors.

Funding

This work was supported by the European Union Programme Horizon 2020 under Grant number 653866 as part of the project 'Whole of Society Conflict Prevention and Peacebuilding'.

[67]Sherriff et al., 'Glass half full', 31.

[68]Julian Bergmann, 'The European Union as a peace mediator', *Sustainable Security* (Blog post, 17 June 2016). See online at: https://sustainablesecurity.org/2016/06/17/the-european-union-as-a-peace-mediator/.

Decentralising power: building inclusive peace? The European Union's support to governance reform in Eastern Ukraine

Matteo Dressler

ABSTRACT

This article contributes to the ongoing debate on what role decentralisation processes can play in building sustainable peace. More specifically, the article reflects upon the European Union's (EU's) support to the implementation of decentralisation reform in government-controlled areas of Eastern Ukraine, examining the EU's support to civil society and local authorities in areas affected by the armed conflict. A Whole-of-Society lens is employed to analyse the topic, paying special attention to connections between multiple levels of relevant actors in the reform process. The final discussion reveals multiple challenges for decentralisation reform in Eastern Ukraine such as insufficient communication by the national government with local authorities and lack of participation of broader segments of society in the process. However, it also shows the reform's potential for empowering local actors to take on issues such as social cohesion and gender violence.

Introduction

Since the end of the Cold War, support to governance reform has risen high on the agenda of peacebuilding and development agencies as an intended method to prevent and transform conflict and enhance democratisation,[1] development and public participation.[2] One type of governance reform, which is often linked with peacebuilding, is decentralisation. A part of current research evidence suggests that decentralisation processes in states affected by conflict are positively associated with a number of conflict-mitigating factors.[3] Decentralisation reform processes can also be linked to the re-emergence of conflicts and a relapse into violence.[4]

---

[1]All online documents were last accessed 19 January 2018, unless otherwise stated.

[2]Markus Schultze-Kraft and Egjellushe Morina, 'Decentralisation and Accountability in War-to-peace Transitions: The Case of Kosovo', *IDS Bulletin* 45, no.5 (2014) 92–104; Mohammad Agus Yusoff, Athambawa Sarjoon and Mat Ali Hassan, 'Decentralization as a Tool for Ethnic Diversity Accommodation: A Conceptual Analysis', *Journal of Politics and Law* 9, no. 1 (2016): 55–64; Wolff, Stefan, 'Conflict Management in Divided Societies: The Many Uses of Territorial Self-Governance', *International Journal on Minority and Group Rights* 20, no. 1 (2013): 27–50.

[3]Joseph Siegle and Patrick O'Mahony, *Assessing the merits of decentralization as a conflict mitigation strategy* (Washington: USAID, 2009); Derick W. Brinkerhoff, 'State Fragility and Governance: Conflict Mitigation and Subnational Perspectives', *Development Policy Review 29*, no. 2 (2011): 131–53.

[4]Dawn Brancati, *Peace by Design: Managing Intrastate Conflict through Decentralization* (Oxford: Oxford University Press, 2009); Arlid Schou and Marit Haug, *Decentralisation in Conflict and Post-Conflict Situations* (Oslo: Norwegian Institute for Urban and Regional Research, 2005).

Inclusion of multiple levels of society and the state is one mechanism which is frequently mentioned in the academic literature and in policy and practitioner communities why governance reforms are more likely to succeed in contributing to building sustainable peace. The validity and controversies of this argument have been tested in depth elsewhere for political settlements, peace processes and governance reform.[5] This article is interested in adding to this debate by exploring how international peacebuilders support inclusion in decentralisation reform and the challenges they encounter.

The European Union (EU) is one international actor that puts governance reform and support to decentralisation at the forefront of its foreign policy. In light of its increasing involvement in the field of conflict prevention and conflict resolution, it has also leveraged decentralisation as a tool – among other interventions – for peacebuilding. Despite some mixed results regarding the success of supporting decentralisation processes, the EU is currently supporting a number of such reforms.[6] The article looks at Eastern Ukraine as one current example in which the EU supports national decentralisation reform as an instrument to support peacebuilding. Special emphasis is placed on the inclusion of civil society and local authorities as part of the decentralisation process and as potential priority groups for EU support. Ukraine as a case is highly relevant since its decentralisation reform is closely linked, both to the armed conflict in the East of the country and the resulting peacebuilding needs in areas close to the contact line of the conflicting parties.[7]

The aim of exploring this case is to develop an understanding of the investigative/analytical potential of the Whole-of-Society (WOS) approach discussed in this special issue.[8] The concept will be used in this article as an analytical lens to order information about the EU's relation and/or support to (ex)included actors in the decentralisation process on different societal levels (national, subnational) and also their (non)coordination and (non)cooperation with each other. Thus, it uses foremost the lower part of the vertical axis of the WOS peacebuilding lens, which generally can be utilised to assess the connection, relationships and (non)coordination or (non)cooperation between the multiple political and societal actors and groups with a stake in a certain peacebuilding endeavour (see Figure 1).

The research question explored in this article is: 'Does the EU support inclusion of civil society and local stakeholder in decentralisation reform, and what are the challenges this support encounters?

The article starts with a short overview on the topic of decentralisation, peacebuilding and inclusion, succeeded by a review of policies for EU support to decentralisation reform. The next section forms the empirical core of the article and presents the EU's support to decentralisation reform in Ukraine. The article continues with an analytical discussion, including an inquiry of the case study through the WOS lens, and ends with a conclusion.

---

[5]Véronique Dudouet and Stina Lundström, 'Post-war Political Settlements: From Participatory Transition Processes to Inclusive State-building and Governance' (Berlin: Berghof Foundation, 2016); Alina Rocha Menocal, 'Inclusive Political Settlements: Evidence, Gaps, and Challenges of Institutional Transformation' (Birmingham, UK: International Development Department, University of Birmingham, 2015).

[6]Per Tidemand, Hans Bjørn Olsen, Philip Bøttern, Emmanuel Pousse and Christiane Loquai, 'Thematic global evaluation of the Commission support to decentralisation processes', *Evaluation for the European Commission (No. 1)* (Brussels: Particip GMBH, 2012).

[7]An EEAS official at headquarters, interviewed by the author in March 2017, also shared this assessment.

[8]Mary Martin, Linda Benrais and Vesna Bojicic-Dzelilovic, 'Introduction' (in this special issue).

Figure 1. Whole-of-Society lens on EU peacebuilding in Ukraine.

The case study on Ukraine is based on interviews with EU and United Nations Development Program (UNDP) officials, both in Brussels and Ukraine[9] conducted both by the author and as part of a research report[10] produced in the frame of the WOSCAP project by the Institute of World Policy in Kiev. It is complimented by information from extensive evaluations and reports on Ukraine's decentralisation reform, which are based on public opinion surveys and a wide range of qualitative interviews with local and national stakeholders from all levels of society, with a focus on a wide social spectrum of respondents.[11]

Decentralisation and (inclusive) peacebuilding

In this article, decentralisation is understood as a principle of 'dispersing political, administrative and/or fiscal powers from the central state to sub-national agencies or

[9]Interviews were conducted with EU delegation officials in Kiev, an EU official of the EEAS' Ukraine country team based in Brussels, UNDP officials based in Kiev, one former member of the OSCE monitoring mission and one NGO worker implementing a grass-roots dialogue project in Luhansk and Donetsk provinces. Furthermore, UNDP Ukraine also provided answers to a questionnaire in writing. Conducting of interviews took place on multiple occasions between summer 2016 and spring 2017. Collection of secondary data ended in January 2018 and the article hence refers to developments before this date.

[10]Leonid Litra, Ivan Medynskyi, Kateryna Zarembo, 'Assessing the EU's conflict prevention and peacebuilding interventions in Ukraine'. http://www.woscap.eu/documents/131298403/131299900/D3.4_Case+Study+Report+Ukraine_PU.pdf/de6f7a64-17d6-4b89-b902-7f0b3284edff.

[11]International Alert and Ukrainian Center for Independent Political Research, 'Decentralisation in Ukraine: Achievements, expectations and concerns' (London: International Alert, 2017). http://www.international-alert.org/sites/default/files/Ukraine_Decentralisation_EN_2017.pdf; International Alert and Ukrainian Center for Independent Political Research, 'Citizens and the state in the government-controlled territories of the Donetsk and Luhansk regions: Problems, challenges and visions of the future' (London: International Alert, 2017). https://www.international-alert.org/sites/default/files/Ukraine_CitizenStateRelations_EN_2017.pdf (accessed 30 May 2018); Tomila Lankina, Claire Gordon and Svitlana Slava, 'Regional Development in Ukraine: Priority Actions in Terms of Decentralization' (Brussels: European Union and the Committee of the Regions, 2017). https://cor.europa.eu/en/documentation/studies/Documents/Regional-Development-Ukraine.pdf; Council of Europe, 'Decentralization and the Reform of Local self-governance: results of the second wave of sociological research' (2016). https://rm.coe.int/CoERMPublicCommonSearchServices/DisplayDCTMContent?documentId=09000016806dcbe2; Peaceful Change initiative, 'Ukraine: A peacebuilding agenda to bridge the divide' (London: Peaceful Change Initiative, 2017). http://www.peacefulchange.org/uploads/1/2/2/7/12276601/ukraine_policy_brief_final_for_print_2.pdf. The two studies by International Alert and the Ukraine Center for Independent Studies are particular important, as they build (combined) on more than 100 local interviewees with a background in civil society, journalism, local administration, IDP's and local residents.

authorities'.[12] Such processes are framed as federalisation, self-governance or different types of autonomy, which often have different conceptual connotations. There are two main strands of motives for decentralisation highlighted in the literature. The first strand concentrates on the linkages between national decentralisation and (dis)integration with a particular focus on dissolving ethnic tension within a country.[13] In peacebuilding and conflict settings this often goes hand in hand with secessionist demands, or claims for some type of self-determination rights, be it autonomy, a special regional status or increased political, administrative and fiscal influence at a regional and/or local level by non-state armed groups and movements in order to address grievances, marginalisation and/or security needs of their (claimed) constituencies.

The second strand sees decentralisation through a lens of development where decentralisation is assumed to have the potential to reinforce local democracy and strengthen efficiency, equity and responsiveness concerning the use of public resources.[14] This notion also resonates with peacebuilders and conflict parties as making the state more representative, responsive and efficient as a way to transform structural marginalisation and exclusion is a common demand from non-state armed groups during armed struggle, as well as an end goal for many peace processes.[15] Against this background, inclusivity and participation on both inter-elite and elite-society levels in peace processes and post-conflict political settlements have gained traction within academia and the peacebuilding community as principles to avoid new conflicts and violence relapse.[16] In this article we will borrow from the second strand of literature and mainly concentrate on analysing inclusivity as a so-called vertical process defined as

> [t]he extent to which larger segments of the population have access to, and influence over, decision making – with a specific emphasis on (previously) marginalised societal sectors who by tradition, culture or history have limited resources and entry points to access, influence and participate in the power infrastructure.[17]

This type of inclusivity can mainly be measured via participation by the above-mentioned groups, but I will also pay attention to how far content-related input into the political process by those actors has been taken on board.

Previous literature that is available on the topic of decentralisation processes provides us with mixed results regarding their actual peacebuilding potential. There is some empirical evidence available supporting the idea that decentralisation reform can have the ability of a conflict mitigating, or in some cases even conflict transformative, effect by increasing public participation (foremost of minority/marginalised groups), changing dynamics in power relations to accommodate local or regional demands and

---

[12] Pippa Norris, 'Federalism and Decentralisation, in *Driving democracy: do power-sharing institutions work?* Ed. Pippa Norris (Cambridge: Cambridge University Press, 2008): 157–185.

Definitions on decentralisation by the European Union are in essence very similar. See for example: European Commission, *Empowering Local Authorities in partner countries for enhanced governance and more effective development*, COM 280 (15 May 2013), 5–6.

[13] Schou and Haug, 'Decentralisation in Conflict'; Brinkerhoff, 'State Fragility and Governance'.

[14] Chanchal K. Sharma, 'Emerging Dimensions of Decentralization Debate in the Age of Glocalization', *MPRA Paper No. 14,337* (2008). https://mpra.ub.uni-muenchen.de/6734/1/decentralization.pdf; Derick W. Brinkerhoff, 'State Fragility and Governance'.

[15] Dudouet and Lundström, *Post-war Political Settlements.*

[16] Dudouet and Lundström, *Post-war Political Settlements;* Menocal, *Inclusive Political Settlements.*

[17] Dudouet and Lundström, *Post-war Political Settlements*, 9.

making the state itself become more representative and responsive to its citizens' needs at the local level.[18] These positive findings are contrasted with empirical-based research showing that decentralisation reform processes have led to further political and social instability or polarisation or in some cases have even caused new conflicts to emerge or old conflicts to re-emerge.[19] First and foremost, the concept of decentralisation itself is often politicised whereby conflicting actors, state and society have different views on what type of powers should be transferred from the central state, how much of these powers should be transferred, where the new administrative boundaries should be drawn and in some cases even what the new administrative and political units should be called.[20] In addition, it is not a given that the government at a decentralised level of administration is more efficient, representative, inclusive and responsive to citizens' needs and grievances.

In sum, the struggles over political, social and economic influence that often emerge during the processes of changing power distribution suggest that decentralisation is not just a neutral, quick fix, technical exercise consisting of strengthening capacities, remodelling formal intra-state and state–society relations, increasing formal participation or strengthening institutions. Decentralisation should thus in this context – and in this article – be primarily regarded as a potentially long-lasting process which (ideally) aims to resolve different degrees and levels of social and/or political conflicts, and as a means to tackle governance inefficiencies by either rearranging power and/or reforming state structures and procedures.

EU support to decentralisation reform

This section will give a brief overview of the 2013 European Commission (EC) communication, which comprises the EU's current strategy for supporting local authorities and decentralisation outside of its borders.[21] It addresses the question of whether an inclusive approach – working with multiple tracks of society and particularly with civil society and local authorities – is reflected in the document.

The underpinning assumption in the 2013 communication is that decentralisation reform is part of a wider approach to territorial governance, which has the potential to increase efficiency of governance, equality and social cohesion.[22] This notion is based on the realisation that '[c]entrally-led, top-down development policies and programmes cannot alone succeed in addressing the complexities of sustainable development and fighting poverty'; and secondly, that '[t]he participation of citizens in decision-making processes that affect their lives and access to accountability mechanisms is fundamental to the promotion of sustainable development and poverty reduction'.[23] Particular emphasis is put on local authorities and their relation with citizens: 'Being closer to

[18]Siegle and O'Mahony, *'Assessing the merits of decentralization'*; Faguet et al., *'Decentralising for Democracy'*; Brinkerhoff, *'State Fragility and Governance'*; Yusoff et al., 'Decentralisation for Ethnic Diversity Accommodation'.

[19]Schou and Haug, 'Decentralisation in Conflict'; Brancati, *Peace by Design*.

[20]Schou and Haug, 'Decentralisation in Conflict'; Derick W. Brinkerhoff, 'State Fragility and Governance'.

[21]European Commission, *Empowering Local Authorities*; also see European Commission, 'Supporting decentralisation, local governance and local development through a territorial approach', *Tools and Methods Series, Reference Document No 23* (Brussels: European Commission, 2016).

[22]European Commission. *Empowering Local Authorities*, 6.

[23]Ibid., 2.

citizens than other public institutions, local authorities hold responsibility in mobilising local societies' opinions while acting as catalysts for change.'[24]

Equipped with this awareness, the step towards making the linkage between decentralisation reform and inclusive and participatory peacebuilding was small. Thus, the 2013 communication makes a clear link to the role local authorities can and should play in conflict prevention, resolution and management. Firstly, it mentions a range of conflict drivers and ramifications which can affect local communities and their local authorities in fragile and conflict-prone/affected places, for example, social exclusion, migration, public safety and violence, rule of law and access to justice, etc.[25] Similarly, it outlines the responsibility of local authorities to protect the local population when faced with imminent conflict or threat, for example by strengthening the resilience of the communities under their rule. It also stresses their role in early warning and de-escalation, for example, through employing traditional dispute resolution mechanisms.[26]

In a nutshell, EU policies and strategies acknowledge a relationship between local communities and conflict prevention and management, and single out decentralisation reform as one of the key drivers to support the capacities of local authorities and communities to deal with such challenges.

The EU's support to Ukraine's decentralisation reform

This section provides information on the EU's capabilities and challenges to support inclusive decentralisation reform in the case of Ukraine.

Ukraine: an intricate setting for political reform support

Ukraine's current process of governance reform started after its proclamation of independence in 1991 and the need for decentralisation reform has been on the Ukrainian political agenda ever since.[27] The document which is currently most central in outlining EU support to decentralisation in Ukraine is the EU Ukraine Association Agenda to prepare and facilitate the implementation of the Association Agreement.[28] The history of the most recent EU support to decentralisation reform in Ukraine is in fact quite intricate. The negotiations around the Association Agreement and the eventual rejection of the agreement by former Ukrainian president Viktor Yanukovych in 2013 led to the mobilisation of Ukrainian pro-EU supporters in 2013 and the so-called Maidan protests. Ultimately, the pressure created by the protests led to Yanukovych's ousting and brought to power a pro-European government under the current president Petro Poroshenko.[29] Taken aback by these developments, Russia –

[24]Ibid., 4.
[25]Ibid., 2.
[26]Ibid., 4.
[27]Litra et al., 'Assessing the EU's conflict prevention'.
[28]EU-Ukraine Association Council, 'EU-Ukraine Association Agenda to prepare and facilitate the implementation of the Association Agreement' (2015). http://eeas.europa.eu/archives/docs/ukraine/docs/st06978_15_en.pdf; European Commission, 'Supporting decentralisation'.
[29]Ireneusz Pawel Karolewski and Maia K. Davis Cross, 'The EUs Power in the Russia-Ukraine Crisis: Enabled or Constrained?', *JCMS: Journal of Common Market Studies* 55, no. 1 (2017): 137–52; David Marples, 'Decentralization: Pros, Cons, and Prospects', in: *Ukraine in Conflict: An Analytical Chronicle* (Bristol: E-International Relations Publishing), 169–176; Litra et al., 'Assessing the EU's conflict prevention'.

which has a crucial geopolitical interest in Ukraine – intervened militarily in Crimea in March 2014 and annexed the Ukrainian peninsula. Subsequently, unrest erupted in the majoritarian Russian-speaking regions of South and Eastern Ukraine in April 2014.

Two main factors contributed to the latter development: firstly, Russia's military and economic support to separatist groups active in the Eastern regions;[30] and secondly, fears among the population caused by long-standing attempts of minimising Russian cultural influence in the East and the proposed policies of the Ukrainian government, which aimed at prohibiting Russian as an official language in the country.[31] Turmoil turned into full-fledged armed conflict and de facto self-governance by independent and pro-Russian rebel forces in parts of Donetsk and Luhansk oblast (region). Despite the violent developments in the East of the country, decentralisation and local self-governance have remained national reform priorities for the government-controlled regions.[32]

Two very different endeavours towards decentralisation are currently ongoing in Ukraine and the occupied territories. The first process is focused on administrative, fiscal and political decentralisation, which aims to make the Ukraine state more efficient. This undertaking is limited to government-controlled territories and works against the background of a highly centralised post-soviet Ukrainian state in which even the smallest of local affairs were coordinated through Kiev, resulting in de facto absent local management.[33] This arrangement was prone to inefficient decision-making, and a decentralisation reform was introduced in 2014 to overcome these shortcomings.[34] Its most significant changes entailed that legislation is still made in Kiev, but regional, district and local governments have the autonomy to implement them, as well as to administrate schools, hospitals and other public services.[35] As part of this reform, an amalgamation process is currently under way. Hence, small communities are being merged into bigger municipalities (*hrormadas*) in order to allow for functional service delivery and local management which corresponds to the newly attained responsibilities at the local level.[36] Furthermore, local elections are taking place in government-controlled territories since late 2015.

In the mould of mitigating armed conflicts through a geographically delimited special status for particular regions, the second decentralisation undertaking in Ukraine concerns federalisation.[37] Hence, it was agreed by the parties to the Minsk II

---

[30] International Crisis Group, 'Russia and the Separatists in Eastern Ukraine', International *Crisis Group Europe and Central Asia Briefing N°79* (Kiev/Brussels: International Crisis Group, 2016).

[31] Anna Matveeva, 'No Moscow Stooges: Identity Polarization and Guerrilla Movements in Donbass', *Southeast European and Black Sea Studies* 16, no. 1 (2016): 25–50; International Crisis Group, 'Ukraine: Running out of Time', *Europe Report N°231* (Brussels: International Crisis Group, 2014).

The law which allows for Russian as an official language in some regions of Ukraine was ultimately not repealed (ibid.)

[32] Litra et al., 'Assessing the EU's conflict prevention'; Lankina et al., 'Regional Development in Ukraine'; Gustav Gressel, 'Keeping up Appearances how Europe is Supporting Ukraine's Transformation' (London: European Council on Foreign Relations, 2016). http://www.ecfr.eu/page/-/ukraine_audit_pdf.pdf.

[33] Gressel, 'Keeping Up Appearances'.

[34] Gressel, 'Keeping Up Appearances'; Marples, 'Decentralization: Pros, Cons'.

[35] Gressel, 'Keeping Up Appearances'.

[36] Lankina et al., 'Regional Development in Ukraine'.

[37] None of the conflicting parties uses the term 'federalisation' at the time of writing. The author uses it to make analytical distinction between the different forms of power devolution that are present in Ukraine. See also Marguerite Marlin, 'Concepts of "Decentralization" and "Federalization" in Ukraine: Political Signifiers or Distinct Constitutionalist Approaches for Devolutionary Federalism?', *Nationalism and Ethnic Politics 22*, no.3, (2016): 278–299.

peace agreement that the non-government-controlled areas[38] would receive a special status which would allow them some type of autonomy and self-governance in their territories. However, the current package of proposed constitutional changes which was drafted as a result of the Minsk agreement mixes clauses on introducing the special status with other changes which are mostly relevant for overall, above described, decentralisation reform.[39] Against this complex background public discourse is often confounding issues related to decentralisation, the special status and claims for independence, or becoming part of Russia in the non-government-controlled territories in Luhansk and Donetsk regions. Due to the difficult security situation, the unstable ceasefire as well as the public repudiation of the current formulation of the special status law on the government-controlled side, it seems highly unlikely that a special status will be put into practice in the near future.[40,41]

The case: the Instrument for Stability and Peace (IcSP)-funded project 'restoration of governance and reconciliation in crisis affected communities of Ukraine'

The EU's engagement in the current processes of decentralisation has many different elements and has been supported through various channels (policy, funding, diplomatic engagement) and is counted as one of the reform priorities in Ukraine by the EU.[42] Given the limited scope of this article, I will mainly focus on one out of multiple substantive decentralisation support initiatives currently being pursued by the EU in Ukraine, the EU's IcSP-funded project 'Restoration of governance and reconciliation in crisis affected communities of Ukraine'. This project is of particular interest due to its strong focus on local peacebuilding. The project is being implemented by UNDP and UN Women in the government-controlled areas closest to the contact line (Luhansk and Donetsk regions). Focus areas of the project which relate directly to peacebuilding are the high concentration of Internally Displaced Persons (IDPs) in government-controlled areas and issues of social cohesion between IDPs and host communities, and the responsibility of local authorities to manage these increasingly tense relations and to coordinate with law enforcement agencies; a lack of social service delivery on the local level with potential to cause further conflict; increased threats of intercommunal and interpersonal violence (particular gender violence) in areas (previously) affected by military conflict and the role of local authorities in addressing these threats.[43] Illustrative of the challenges is the response by a local resident who lives close to the contact line in government-controlled areas and reflects on relations between IDP's and the local population.

[38]Referred to as individual areas of the Donetsk and Luhansk regions in the Minsk Agreements.
[39]Lankina et al., 'Regional Development in Ukraine'.
[40]Marples, 'Decentralization: Pros, Cons'; The Economist, 'What are the Minsk agreements?' *The Economist*, 16 September 2016. http://www.economist.com/blogs/economist-explains/2016/09/economist-explains-7; Gwendolyn Sasse, 'The Donbas – Two parts, or still one? The experience of war through the eyes of the regional population', *ZOiS Report 2/2017* (Berlin: Centre for East European and International Studies, 2017). https://www.zois-berlin.de/fileadmin/media/Dateien/ZOiS_Reports/ZOiS_Report_2_2017.pdf .
[41]An EEAS official at headquarters, interviewed by the author in March 2017, also shared this assessment of challenges.
[42]Phone interview with EEAS official at headquarters in March 2017.
[43]UNDP. 2016a. 'Restoration of Governance and Reconciliation in Crisis-Affected Communities of Ukraine', *Project leaflet*. http://www.ua.undp.org/content/dam/ukraine/docs/Donbas/Leaflet_UN_Women.pdf.

> … you need to take into account the general tensions. On weekdays, as a rule, hundreds of people come from that territory [from the non-government controlled areas], with certain moods, with a certain emotional background. They crowd into our social services and shops. It seems as if everything is all right. But on the other hand, it is very difficult to emotionally survive all this. Especially in overcrowded social security departments where people queue for hours. After that, there is no desire to smile at them or enjoy life. They come here embittered.[44]

The urgent need to tackle issues related to peacebuilding even during the ongoing conflict in Ukraine arises as there is no immediate solution to the current situation in sight, whereas there is also no full-blown war ongoing (not diminishing the disastrous impact of frequent skirmishes along the contact line).[45]

Against the background of decentralisation and territorial reform, which will strongly impact the work of local institution in the target area, the project's goals are spelled out as follows:

> The project will strengthen the capacity of the local and regional authorities to develop policies, plans and budgets that are based on gender analysis and responsive to the needs of women, men, girls and boys. In addition, the project will ensure equal and meaningful participation by women and men, particularly the most vulnerable, in the decision-making process.[46]

Furthermore, it states the assumption that decentralisation in concert with other factors (recovery, social cohesion, security) can play a crucial role in preventing further conflict in the region. Several mechanisms such as improved service delivery, conflict-sensitive governance and intra- and intercommunity dialogue as part of the decentralisation process are emphasised for their potential to link decentralisation with peacebuilding.[47]

The EU's support for decentralisation reform in Ukraine: an inclusive endeavour?

The project started its implementation phase in May 2016 and ran for 18 months with a budget of EUR 10 million.[48] The project design process was based on regional development plans which were created by local authorities (from oblast, rayon and city level) and civil society from the region with support from UNDP.[49] In these plans priorities for local and regional development are formulated. The plans also form the basis for receiving subsidies from the national government in the framework of giving more financial responsibilities to regional and local authorities. As one UNDP official states:

> Because the regional administration engaged in a participatory consultative process with working groups in four areas to discuss these things from bottom up [… it] actually produce[d] a very different type of regional strategy document [different] from the usual convoluted, very technocratic documents that nobody would ever read. This is actually designed to be read by an interesting public and should be considered as owned by the communities. And this was very useful because, for instance, the emphasis on community

[44]International Alert 2017, 'Citizens and the state', 24.
[45]Phone interview with EEAS official at headquarters in March 2017; also see Peaceful Change initiative, 'Ukraine: A peacebuilding agenda'.
[46]UNDP. 2016a. 'Restoration of Governance'.
[47]Ibid.
[48]18 months is the maximum duration for IcSP-funded projects that aim at rapid response and flexible programming.
[49]Litra et al., 'Assessing the EU's conflict prevention'.

> security, and administrative reform, and IDPs and social cohesion are also the themes that we integrated into the proposal and, therefore, now the action [the project]. So what we now have is that we have a government-owned product of a participatory process, which is this regional development strategy, and we have the resources from the EU to actually conduct the targeted programmes in those areas. [50]

Based on these regional development plans, the project was jointly drawn up by the EU delegation to Ukraine the UNDP and its implementing partners, while the IcSP was foremost involved in its funding.[51] On the down side, as the UNDP's inception report from October 2016 states, a planned follow-up on the development strategy being jointly conducted by the Swedish International Development Cooperation Agency and the Swiss Agency for Development and Cooperation was lacking the funds (at that point) for conducting consultations, presenting an issue for the timely adaptation of the project to local and regional developments.[52]

During the early phase the project particularly benefited from the long-standing field presence by the EU's implementing partner UNDP in the geographic areas covered by the project.[53] In combination with established expertise of supporting governance reform in Ukraine by both the EU and UNDP, this meant that contacts and working relationships with local stakeholders were already established and that, for example, the UNDP had a pre-existing regional headquarters from which it could start implementing the project.[54] Based on these relationships, UNDP has, for example, undertaken broad public consultations with both local administrations and local civil society organisations[55] with a focus on reconciliation and social cohesion initiatives in order to both inform them and develop with them a monitoring tool aimed at creating an evidence base on inter-group relations. This tool will serve to inform UNDP's work on social cohesion and support Ukrainian local authorities to improve their governance intervention in that field through a more sophisticated evidence base.[56]

From a perspective of vertical inclusivity, two other points are worth mentioning. Firstly, although the current project is not able to cover the non-government-controlled territories in Donetsk and Luhansk at this point, the UNDP was chosen by the EU as an implementing partner based on the perception of its neutrality and impartially and thus its potential acceptance by all actors to work in these areas, should the conflict environment change in the future.[57] Currently the EU refrains from engaging in the occupied territories for a number of reasons, including the security situation[58] and the

[50]UNDP official interviewed in Kiev 2016, for Litra et al., 'Assessing the EU's conflict prevention', 60.

[51]Phone interview with EEAS official at headquarters in March 2017. The full list of official partners in Ukraine can be found here: http://www.ua.undp.org/content/ukraine/en/home/operations/projects/recovery-and-peacebuilding/restoration-and-reconciliation-eu.html (accessed 30 May 2018).

[52]UNDP. 2016b. 'Inception Report: Restoration of Governance and Reconciliation in Crisis-affected Communities of Ukraine' (2016: 12). http://www.ua.undp.org/content/ukraine/en/home/operations/projects/recovery-and-peacebuilding/restoration-and-reconciliation.html.

[53]Ibid.; Litra et al., 'Assessing the EU's conflict prevention'.

[54]Litra et al., 'Assessing the EU's conflict prevention'.

[55]'regional administrations and a wide range of local civil society organizations – about 60 participants in total' (UNDP. 2016b. 'Inception Report',19).

[56]Ibid. 19–20.

[57]Phone interview with EEAS official at headquarters in March 2017; Interview with a UNDP official, Kiev, 2016 for Litra et al., 'Assessing the EU's conflict prevention.

[58]Phone interview with EEAS official at headquarters in March 2017. For more information on the security situation: OSCE Special Monitoring Mission to Ukraine, *Hardship for conflict-affected civilians in eastern Ukraine*, Thematic Report (OSCE Publishing, 2017). http://www.osce.org/ukraine-smm/300276?download=true.

fact that it would not be granted access by authorities in the occupied areas. Secondly, the current project has a strong gender component, which is being implemented by UN Women. Thus, whereas the whole project has a cross-cutting gender focus, two million of the overall EUR 10 million budget were specifically earmarked for the gender component. The participation of UN Women was facilitated by the EU delegation in Ukraine.[59] A concrete example of their work was the input gathered for the regional development plans by a range of 16 women's organisations, as well as female leaders on the different levels of regional administration. These were intended to get the input by and increase the influence of women on local decision-making on recovery, planning and budgeting and community security.[60]

Next to the EU's internal capacities, a range of external factors shape the context in which the decentralisation process in Ukraine takes place. Next to the fluid security context, the problem of adapting the necessary legal framework for decentralisation reform on the national level poses a problem. Particularly the stalling of parts of the decentralisation reform in the national parliament implies that local authorities without a clear legislative framework carry out many of the reform's aspects.[61] What also seems to be particularly challenging regarding the EU's engagements is the politicisation of the decentralisation issue. While polls show that the western parts of Ukraine are largely in favour of the reforms, the picture is less favourable in government-controlled territories close to the contact line.[62] In any case, supporting such a politically loaded reform bears the risk for the EU of being perceived as partisan. This is particularly valid since public opinion in the Donbass is generally less favourable to EU integration than the rest of the country.[63]

Moreover, support to decentralisation reform also works in a context of existing power structures. One example is that local authorities are resisting restructuring of districts in parts of the country as they face a loss of power.[64] Furthermore, decentralisation threatens the power of oligarchic structures –comprising a business elite which became very rich through economic liberalisation policies after the fall of the Soviet Union – which fear to loose influence to newly strengthened local authorities.[65] Conflict about power between these groups is also one of the main public concerns.[66] Another and related issue, hampering decentralisation on the local levels, is corruption.[67] Powerful economic players often use corruption to influence local media to manipulate political public opinion to their benefits. Together with irregularities during elections, this impedes the motivation by citizens to engage or participate in formal local politics.[68] The UNDP project acknowledges these structural issues and

[59]Interview with an EU Delegation official, Kiev, 2016, for Litra et al, 'Assessing the EU's conflict prevention', 58.
[60]UNDP. 2016a. 'Restoration of Governance'.
[61]Lankina et al., 'Regional Development in Ukraine'; International Alert, 'Decentralisation in Ukraine'.
[62]Council of Europe 2016, 'Reform of Local self-governance', 29pp.
[63]Ilko Kucheriv Democratic Initiatives Foundation, 'Public opinion in Donbas: July 2017' (2017), 3, 9. http://dif.org.ua/uploads/pdf/7122114865989998d61e272.26298946.pdf.
[64]International Alert, 'Decentralisation in Ukraine'.
[65]Olena Makarenko, 'Decentralization: the mortal threat to Ukraine's entrenched elites', *Euro Maidan Press*, 11 November 2017. http://euromaidanpress.com/2017/11/07/decentralization-the-mortal-threat-to-ukraines-entrenched-elites/; Andrew Wilson, 'Survival of the Richest: How Oligarchs Block Reform in Ukraine', *Policy Brief.* (European Council on Foreign Relations, 2016).
[66]Lankina et al., 'Regional Development in Ukraine'.
[67]Ibid.
[68]Ibid.

has built in anti-corruption component with capacity building measures for community monitoring of publicly funded projects, integrity measures and capacity building for tracking financial flows, etc.[69] Nevertheless, breaking the ties between powerful economic players and political power holders to prevent or substantially lower their chances to take illegal influence will be a long-term process.[70]

Another issue that the decentralisation process is facing is the difficulty to motivate people to participate and give input:

> During 70 years of living in the Soviet Union, our people got used to having someone tell them what to do and how to live. No one wants to solve problems on their own [...] we need to work not only with the authorities, but with the local communities [so] that the residents of districts and regions understand that their involvement [...] could change the situation [...].[71]

A handling of decisions, with a 'tendency of paternalism' by local authorities, foments this rather passive habitus, scepticism towards authorities and a lack of exercising citizen rights.[72] As a study on relations between the citizens and state shows, this phenomenon is particularly prominent in Donetsk and Luhansk regions.[73]

This is contrasted by the observation that people on local level close to the contact line are often primarily concerned with immediate needs rather than political reform.[74] An interview response by a resident who lives close to the contact line illustrates that well:

> We have problems like all Ukrainians, like everyone else. Utility prices, gas prices. We pay 3,000 [hryvnya] a month for gas. Our parents cannot pay, they have applied for a subsidy, they have been waiting a long time. The queues are huge, you see what is going on in Volnovakha.[75]

Thus, as many respondents in a study on public perception of the decentralisation process stressed, a range of tools were available for public participation for shaping the amalgamation of districts. The challenge was rather to engage regular citizens in those processes, and to familiarise them with mechanism of public participation, and the respective decision-making procedures in general.[76]

Next to the more obvious challenges such as a lack of funds bemoaned by local authorities,[77] one of the key bottlenecks for successful decentralisation is the poor communication strategy by the central government with its lower levels of state authority on the process. This shortcoming leads to perceived ambiguities and even bickering over the distribution of tasks, funds and power between the different local levels.[78] This is well epitomised in a quote from a paper studying success of

---

[69]UNDP. 2016b. 'Inception Report',16–18.
[70]Lankina et al., 'Regional Development in Ukraine'.
[71]Interviewee in Kiev, in: International Alert, 'Decentralisation in Ukraine', 13.
[72]International Alert, 'Citizens and the state', 17.
[73]Ibid., 6.
[74]Interview by the authors with a staff member of an international NGO who works on grassroots training in dialogue and mediation for people close to the contact line.
[75]Interview with local resident in Volnovakha for International Alert (2017) 'Citizens and the state', 23.
[76]International Alert, 'Citizens and the state'.
[77]However, the budget did significantly increase over the last three years: Council of Europe, 'Achievements of decentralisation in Ukraine presented at the Council of Europe' 6 February 2017. https://www.coe.int/en/web/kyiv/-/achievements-of-decentralisation-in-ukraine-presented-at-the-council-of-europe.
[78]Lankina et al., 'Regional Development in Ukraine'.

decentralisation reform in Ukraine as a whole: 'There was the fear that we would lose a village council after the amalgamation. No village council, no village. No school, no village. It is time to dispel these myths.'[79] These challenges are more acute in the East of the country, and the municipalities closest to the conflict. Hence, only 37% of the local population in the East of the country believes that the reform will improve the development of communities compared to an average of 51% in the rest of Ukraine.[80] Additionally, it is interesting to see that optimism of improvement for community development is positively related with how well respondents are informed about the reform (e.g. among those who know nothing 33% expect improvement of community development, while the number for well-informed respondents is 69%).[81] In sum, although some of the negative prejudices disappeared after municipalities were directly engaged in restructuring efforts related to reform,[82] it shows the need for constant outreach and education about the ongoing reform processes as the following quote by a regional development expert on decentralisation shows:

> People lack information. The authorities are not interested in providing them with information. I mean the chairpersons of village councils ... People do not understand what is going on, what actions they have to take, what they are responsible for, and what they need to do.[83]

Applying a WOS lens

This section returns to the question outlined in the introduction, whether the EU supports the inclusion of civil society and local stakeholders in decentralisation reform in Eastern Ukraine and which challenges attach to this support? It uses the previous section as an empirical backdrop for an analytical discussion guided by a WOS lens.

Using the vertical axis to assess inclusivity in decentralisation reform in Eastern Ukraine

The review of the main policy documents on EU decentralisation support revealed that the EU clearly outlined the peacebuilding dimensions of decentralisation reform and identified it as critical to increase governance efficiency, equality and social cohesion in (post-)conflict contexts. Concurring with the definition of vertical process inclusivity – 'the extent to which larger segments of the population have access to, and influence over, decision making' – the EU also aims to support local authorities and harness their potential to bring in the input by local civil society. This argumentation closely resembles the decentralisation strand of literature discussed earlier in this article, which stresses development and progress of local democracy as mechanisms improving government responsiveness and thereby contributing to peacebuilding.

For the case of Eastern Ukraine, the choice of a funding instrument designed to support peace and stability for the above-examined project shows that the EU does

---

[79]Interview in Dnipro, in: International Alert, 'Decentralisation in Ukraine', 10.
[80]Council of Europe 2016, 'Reform of Local self-governance', 46.
[81]ibid. 49.
[82]International Alert, 'Decentralisation in Ukraine'.
[83]Interview in Kiev, Ibid. 17.

make the link between decentralisation and peacebuilding not only in its policy documents, but also in its practical support. Regarding the support to vertical inclusion, the EU based the main priorities of the project on development plans written by local authorities with the participation of civil society groups. Furthermore, the objectives of the project emphasise the inclusion of civil society and women. In the early phase of the project, these objectives had materialised, for example, in support to collecting the input by female local leaders (in both civil society and local authorities) for an update of regional development plans.

On the other hand, a range of issues complicated the current decentralisation process, as well as the promotion of vertical inclusivity for the EU. For example, the inclusion of local stakeholders into the decentralisation process works against the background of a historically conditioned lack of experience with democratic governance structures on the local level as well as a passive habitus concerning civic engagement in political reform. Although civil society engagement has clearly and rapidly increased after the Maidan protests,[84] it still takes place in an overall context of scepticism regarding citizen engagement that is deeply ingrained in wide segments of society, particularly in the Donbas. This feeling is only fomented by a lack of knowledge of mechanisms of how to engage by many regular citizens. Such contexts, and the practices it brings about (or does not bring about in terms of engagement), might only change over a long period, far beyond the reach of international organisation's project cycles. Whereas the limited scope of his essay does not allow for any big conclusions, its findings confirm some of the challenges pointed out in the strand of literature on political transitions, which deals with the difficulties of consolidating an inclusive political culture.[85] In other words, this article illustrates some of the challenges of forming a vibrant democratic civil society, which, ideally, can act as a counterbalancing force to political and economic power players.[86] Secondly, it describes the complex task of co-creating democratic institutions through which citizens feel that their values and attitudes are reflected.[87]

Visualising the above points along the vertical axis of the WOS lens, they mostly focus on the relationship between the EU (as a regional power engaged in governance reform and peacebuilding) and its support, and challenges of support to the subnational state level under the inclusion of civil society and the crosscutting group of women. In addition, the case study has shown the lack of a good enough communication strategy by the national government (which links national and subnational level within the lens) and its potential to spoil the efforts to support reform. Hence, lack of information has led to public speculations and stereotype of negative aspects of the reform. This deficit might be reinforced by the prevalence of extremely wealthy business elites with the

[84]Olga Burlyuk and Natalia Shapovalova, 'Ukraine's Civic Progress and Partial Reform', 8 January 2018. Carnegie. https://carnegieendowment.org/2018/01/08/ukraine-s-civic-progress-and-partial-reform-pub-75181 (accessed 30 May 2018).

[85]Wolfgang Merkel, *Systemtransformation. Eine Einführung in die Theorie und Empirie der Transformationsforschung* (Wiesbaden: VS Verlag für Sozialwissenschaften, 2010); Hans-Joachim Giessmann and Roger Mac Ginty (eds.), *The Elgar Companion to Post-Conflict Transition* (Cheltenham, UK/ Northampton, USA: Edward Elgar Publishing, 2018 forthcoming); Juan J. Linz and Alfred Stepan, *Problems of Democratic Transition and Consolidation: Southern Europe, South America, and Post-Communist Europe* (Baltimore: Johns Hopkins University Press, 1996).

[86]This article does not leave space for discussion for debates about civil society with democratic or undemocratic objectives. See, for example, Briony Jonesa and Dit Fatogoma Adou Djané, 'Reading the "uncivil" in civil society resistance to transitional justice in Côte d'Ivoire', *Political Geography*, in press.

[87]Merkel 2010, 'System transformation', coins this civic culture.

means and potential interest to float wrong ideas about reforms to preserve their influence on the local level. By linking the regional/global (EU) with the national and subnational, the WOS lens allows thinking those well-known issues of local power struggles and the scarcity of sufficient information and exchange between national and subnational administration together. It reveals the significance of spreading accurate information, in this particular case with the help of support of an external donor. It also re-emphasised the obvious, hence, that understanding political culture (e.g. scepticism towards authorities, sometimes inaction) will largely need to guide what kind of action is needed (e.g. in the form of dialogues or participatory formats) and which limits there are for engaging citizens. In short, thinking in terms of a multilevel vertical axis has helped the author to cluster information and think them together in a more systematic way.

Furthermore, it has helped the author, to see more graphically, what is left outside of his zooming into the vertical axis. The ongoing hostilities in the Donbass region as well as a lack of a (successful) negotiation process to stop violence, or find a political solution for the future role of the currently occupied territories, means that decentralisation reform is not implemented in those territories. Consequently, there is a lack of inputs from this part of the country into the current reform process. This is likely to mean that the realities of populations across the conflict divide will continue to develop differently. Hence, in the occupied territories the distribution of Russian passports, the introduction of the ruble as currency, renationalisation of companies and an end to most trade relationships with mainland Ukraine ties it closer to Russia over time. Therefore, the inclusion of those groups will become more challenging as the situation drags on.[88] In terms of the vertical axis, this part of society can (for now) be pictured as an excluded group and not part of the vertical axis, suggesting that the lens is only partial, reduced by the physical barriers generated by armed conflict.[89]

This article has focused on exploring the EU's support to inclusivity in decentralisation reform through a WOS lens, utilising its vertical axis to order information, describing connections between the EU and the Ukrainian subnational, as well as in-between the national and subnational level. Potential lies in broadening the analysis even further through upper parts of the vertical axis, as well as the horizontal axis. For the former, in the case of the EU, this would analyse coordination with other international actors in peacebuilding interventions and support. It could also delve deeper into the international dimension of the conflict (situated on the upper vertical axis), which hampers the overall process of decentralisation. Hence, Russia's influence on 'every facet of decision making'[90] in the non-government-controlled areas in the East implies that it seeks the greatest possible autonomy and decision-making power for non-government-controlled areas for any future peaceful solution to the current armed conflict in order to keep its political influence.[91] This complicates the discourse on decentralisation in the Ukrainian public and parliament, making it a highly politicised

[88]Peaceful Change initiative, 'Ukraine: A peacebuilding agenda'; Sasse, 'The Donbas'.

[89]Relationship between the two territories of course exists, not the least through a large amount of people crossing the border between the territories. However, this contact does not explicitly relate to decentralisation reform (Peaceful Change initiative, 'Ukraine: A peacebuilding agenda', 3).

[90]Roxana Cristescu and Denis Matveev, 'The challenge of inclusiveness in the peace process in Ukraine', Civil Society Dialogue Network (CSDN) Background Paper (Brussels: EPLO, 2017), 7.

[91]Marlin, 'Concepts of Decentralization in Ukraine'.

topic with connotations of (Russian) security threats and issues of national sovereignty.[92] This trend also resonates with previous arguments in decentralisation literature that decentralisation can further polarise already divided societies.[93] Moreover, it adds to the debate if sequencing complex governance-related measures, such as decentralisation reform, before stable ceasefires is of great value, or if stability, or increased diplomatic efforts should take priority.[94] International Dialogue experts interviewed for a study[95] on grass-roots level dialogues tackling social conflicts in Ukraine bemoaned the same, lamenting that the international community is focusing too much on problem-solving dialogues. Putting the main focus on 'technical issues' such as integrating IDPs, inclusion of civil society in decision-making and implementing decentralisation suggests, the study[96] argues, shying away from the main issue, a political conflict with Russia. Whereas this essay has argued that the above is not solely a technical exercise, the interviewed experts[97] importantly point out 'the elephant in the room', and the influence it has, on the current slow progress and challenges of decentralisation reform in Donetsk and Luhansk oblast.[98]

In relation to the WOS grid, these last observations also show the potential of the horizontal axis of the lens, which can help to order information related to – and comprehend the linkage of – multiple interventions and actions located in different fields of practice and policy concerned with decentralisation reform (e.g. security, development, social cohesion, democratic reform).

Conclusion

The decentralisation process in Eastern Ukraine shows potential for addressing major peacebuilding issues by stimulating vertical inclusivity of reforms: for instance, by working on IDPs and social cohesion, including gender violence into the agenda of capacitating local authorities, and reorganising local service delivery. In this sense, inclusivity can contribute to peacebuilding goals such as reducing marginalisation of certain population groups, grievances arising from neglect of the regions and communities by the central state, and rebuilding communities after conflict. The article has shown that the EU shares this sentiments and uses it as purpose for support. However, the WOS-guided analysis in this article has also revealed some significant challenges for the reform: a disconnect between national and subnational levels as well as between government-controlled and rebel held areas of the Donbass; the salience of corruption and a lack of broad public participation which may be ultimately significant in achieving positive impacts from decentralisation; and lastly potential for discourse around decentralisation reform to cause further polarisation. The essay hence shares with previous literature the mixed results on the potential of decentralisation to contribute

[92]Cristecu and Matveev, 'Challenges of Inclusiveness'; Marples, 'Decentralization: Pros, Cons'; Sasse, 'The Donbas'.
[93]See for example: Brancati, *Peace by Design*.
[94]These different dimensions must of course not follow in sequence, or exclude each other. For more on this debate, see, for example, Roland Paris and Timothy Sisk (eds), The Dilemmas of Statebuilding: Confronting the Contradictions of Postwar Peace Operations (New York: Routledge, 2009).
[95]Tatiana Kyselova, Anne Isabel Kraus, Lars Kirchhoff, Julia von Dobeneck, 'Track three Dialogues in Ukraine', Research Report (CPM and Jean Monnet Centre of Excellence in European Studies, 2017).
[96]Ibid.
[97]Ibid.
[98]On slow progress see International Alert 'Citizens and the state', 17.

to peacebuilding. The early stage of the reform in Ukraine and the fluid security context do not allow any more generic conclusion on the reform's potential for conflict transformation.

Beyond an academic utilisation, the analytical lens used in this article could potentially also be used to conduct assessments for governance reforms which are built on the EU's integrated approach. Discourses such as the EU Global Security Strategy's call for 'a multi-dimensional approach' through the use of all available policies and instruments aimed at conflict prevention, management and resolution',[99] and thus reflect directly the analytical intent of the horizontal axis. Where EU strategy stresses coordination with international agencies and inclusion of the local level,[100] the vertical axis offers analytical potential for thinking about multiple actors in peacebuilding.

Acknowledgments

The author would like to express gratitude to the multitude of people who gave input and commented on this paper: Dr Susan Stewart, Dr Oliver Wolleh, Stina Lundström, Lukasz A. Mackiewicz, Dr Shyamika Jayasundara, Dr Mary Martin, Sergiy Solodkyy, Janel B. Galvanek, Dr Véronique Dudouet, Izzat Khushbakov, Prof Dr Dr Hans-Joachim Giessmann and Dr Vesna Bojicic-Dzelilovic.

Disclosure statement

No potential conflict of interest was reported by the author.

Funding

The research for the article was conducted as part of the project Whole of Society Conflict Prevention and Peacebuilding (WOSCAP), funded by the EU's Horizon 2020 Research and Innovation Programme, Grant agreement no. 653866.

[99]European Union, *EU Global Strategy*, 28.
[100]Ibid.18, 29, 31.

Wholly local? ownership as philosophy and practice in peacebuilding interventions

Vesna Bojicic-Dzelilovic and Mary Martin

ABSTRACT

This paper engages with the theme of local ownership in peacebuilding from a practice-based perspective which suggests that the way in which the external actors reach out and work with local constituencies shows conceptual and practice gaps that limit the applicability of local ownership in day-to-day peacebuilding operations. We examine how, in the case of EU peacebuilding policies, such gaps impair the potential for effective, inclusive and sustainable peacebuilding. Using a whole-of-society (WOS) lens, the paper demonstrates how current modalities of EU engagement fail to embrace the diversity of local society and its authentic forms of mobilisation and action in order to pursue peacebuilding objectives that resonate with locally relevant forms of peace. The paper further reflects on how WOS perspective can provide pointers for enhancing peacebuilding practices in this area.

Introduction

The norm of local ownership of peacebuilding and post-conflict reconstruction goes to the heart of the moral and practical dilemmas of external interventions in civil conflict. The translation from policy ideal to good practice has been observed as a challenge dogged by conceptual confusion and process issues that continue to intrigue scholarship and defy effective implementation. While an emphasis on local agency and empowerment is seen as a critical and often elusive factor in ensuring effective and sustainable peacebuilding by major actors such as the UN and the EU and has featured strongly in reviews of practice (most recently the UN peacekeeping reviews and the EU global strategy), changes are being pursued predominantly at the strategic level whereas tactical and operational difficulties in implementing local ownership persist.[1]

In this paper, we start from the assumption that the practice, or problem-solving perspective of local ownership, represents the most significant deficit which undermines the normative premise of local ownership that it serves to improve the legitimacy of intervention, ensure the increased involvement and support of local populations, and from

---

[1]Antonia Does, *Inclusivity and Local Perspectives in Peacebuilding: Issues, Lessons, Challenges* (Geneva: Dag Hammarskjold Foundation, 2013), http://www.gsdrc.org/document-library/inclusivity-and-local-perspectives-in-peacebuilding-issues-lessons-challenges/; Caroline Hughes, Joakim Öjendal and Isabell Schierenbeck, 'The Struggle versus the Song – The Local Turn in Peacebuilding: An Introduction', *Third World Quarterly* 36, no. 5 (2015): 817–24.

this enhance durable outcomes from international peacebuilding policies. Following the observation that practice also lags scholarship on this issue,[2] this paper attempts to reflect the practice implications of the scholarly debate which has problematised the gap between rhetorical commitment and results on the ground, by showing local engagement as essentially a strategy of compliance with externally promoted policy blueprints, and second as failure to understand 'the local'. We seek to build on these conceptualisations to suggest that the practice deficit not only needs to address both these elements but also tailor implementation more closely to the variegated and dynamic nature of local society at the non-state level, seeing these as creative possibilities and capabilities of external peacebuilding and not a limitation and block on its progress. We propose that a thicker[3] form of engagement with local society based on alignments between external policies on the one hand and non-state actors, networked relationships and subnational processes on the other could address the lag between scholarship and practice.

This is the proposition of a whole-of-society (WOS) approach (Figure 1). In the case of local ownership, WOS extrapolates from scholarship to capture local agency and capabilities that shape the dynamics of peacebuilding processes and their outcomes. A WOS approach would seek to build 'the social capital of intervention'[4] by externals, focusing on leveraging the presence of a diversity of local groups and their networked and agential character in dense

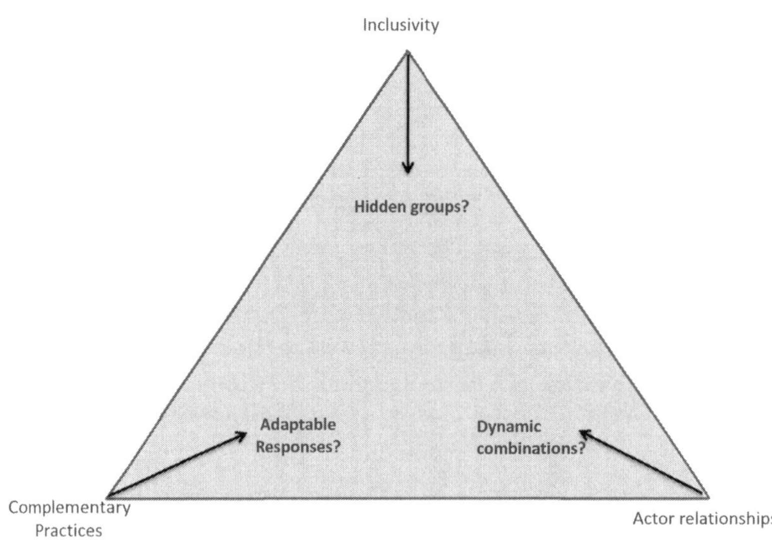

Figure 1. Whole-of-society perspective on local ownership.

[2]Timothy Donais, 'Operationalizing Local Ownership', in *Local Ownership* in *International Peacebuilding: Key Theoretical and Practical Issues*, ed. Sung Yong Lee and Alpaslan Özerdem (Abingdon, New York: Routledge, 2015): 39–55; Cedric de Coning, 'Understanding Peacebuilding as Essentially Local', *Stability* 2, no. 1 (2013): 1–6; Oliver Richmond, 'Beyond Local Ownership in the Architecture of International Peacebuilding', *Ethnopolitics* 11, no. 4 (2012): 354–5; and Caroline Hughes, Joakim Öjendal and Isabell Schierenbeck, 'The Struggle versus the Song'.

[3]Tobias Debiel, Thomas Held and Urlich Schneckener, eds., *Peacebuilding in Crisis: Rethinking Paradigms and Practices of Transnational Cooperation* (Abigdon: Routledge, 2016); and Bridget M. Moix, 'Choosing Peace: Local Peacebuilder Perspectives on Agency, Relational Responsibility, and the Future of International Peacebuilding' (PhD diss., George Mason University, 2016), www/mars.gmu.edu.

[4]A similar idea of a social capital of peacebuilding as a relational resource emanating from peace agency is elaborated by Bridget M. Moix, 'Choosing Peace'.

social contexts of conflict spaces. In peacebuilding terms, social capital emanates within group interactions and co-operation initiatives and in the engagements between external and local constituencies, for example where the EU or other entities fund, enable and empower local actors, providing the 'glue which facilitates, co-operation exchange and innovation' while also accounting for the tensions and contradictions such interactions may entail.[5]

Empirically, we show how local actors mobilise to respond to multiple vulnerabilities they experience and decide on priorities, as well as their flexibility and ability to tap into diverse local capacities. Within a framework of WOS, we also show how local mobilisations respond to opportunities and constraints that international involvement creates. The aim is to suggest new avenues for external engagement which are grounded in both actor and process dynamics within local society. We have grouped these avenues of engagement in terms of (actor) inclusivity, leveraging local relationships and synchronising with practices of local peacebuilding. We suggest that these forms and avenues of engagement constitute latent possibilities of current peacebuilding practice, which can complement and enrich the international-local interaction.

The paper aims to contribute to debates on local ownership by providing a practice-based perspective and by adding to the pool of empirical evidence on the implementation of local ownership at operational level. The analysis draws primarily from empirical data collected during field work in Ukraine in September 2016, which involved a roundtable discussion with local and international practitioners, policymakers, academic experts and civil society activists, 11 individual semi-structured interviews with the representatives of the business sector, faith groups, civil society, informal groups providing humanitarian aid to occupied territories, think tanks and academic experts in Kiev and 1 focus group with civil society organisations. These data are combined with empirical observations from other cases of international interventions in peacebuilding and conflict resolution collected as part of the research project on EU Civilian Capabilities in Conflict Prevention and Peacebuilding and through desk studies.

Local ownership: conceptual–practical contention and the value added of a WOS approach

A recurrent theme among scholars of peacebuilding and development during the last 25 years, local ownership has gone through several iterations of conceptual development whose consequences for peacebuilding practice have been ambivalent at best. In the mid-1990s, the main preoccupation was with a problem of noncompliance with externally supported programmes and policies among the intended beneficiaries of peacebuilding efforts. A lack of take-up and affiliation was attributed to a combination of local resistance to externally prescribed programmes and the fact that policies had limited relevance to realities on the ground, as well as to absent capacities on the recipient side.[6] Questions were raised about how to fix the gaps between the rhetoric

[5]OECD Insights: Human Capital p102 https://www.oecd.org/insights/37966394.pdf. N.d.

[6]Jens Narten, 'Dilemmas of Promoting "Local Ownership" in the Case of Post-war Kosovo', in *The Dilemmas of Statebuilding: Confronting the Contradictions of Postwar Peace Operations*, ed. Roland Paris and Timothy D. Sisk (London, New York; Routledge, 2009), 252–85; and Hannah Reich, 'Local Ownership' in Conflict Transformation Projects: Partnership, Participation or Patronage?' (Berghof Occasional Paper 27, Berlin: Berghof Research Center for Constructive Conflict Management 2006).

and practice of local ownership and, in particular, what was needed to bring about greater engagement of the beneficiaries of international interventions.[7]

Scholarly attempts to address the latter by injecting more clarity and practical utility into the concept of local ownership by pairing it with a range of synonyms, namely participation, inclusion, consultation, dialogue, self-reliance, responsibility and accountability, turned ultimately into an exercise akin to unpacking a Russian doll. Some of those concepts, notably inclusion and participation which became themselves new norms in peacebuilding, proved no less difficult to operationalise.[8] On the interveners' side, the implementation of local ownership with such variable meanings was challenged by a myriad of practical and process issues. These included the difficulties of coordination in a multi-actor peacebuilding context, the prevailing organisational silo mentality, poor operational guidelines, international actors' pragmatic, short-term stabilisation outlook with a focus on discrete (preferably quantifiable) outputs, a lack of sustained effort and more generally the tensions created by approaching essentially political issues in a technocratic manner. For example, a commitment to more participation clashed with a pressure for more control, stricter reporting and donor accountability that practitioners faced.[9] But all together, those practical and process issues were confounded by a lack of conceptual clarity regarding the local of peacebuilding interventions and the meaningful content of the peacebuilding exercise ingrained in the notion of local ownership. The UN and the EU for instance approached local ownership as primarily about engaging with national government elites in contrast to international non-governmental organisations' focus on the societal grass-root level and its actors. As to the substance of peacebuilding, it reflected the interveners' liberal peace variant of market, democracy and good governance as a way to resolve the conflict and sustain peace.[10] Various interpretations of local ownership aside,[11] 'implementing' it on the ground was characterised by partial, superficial, often shallow and ad hoc engagement with a predefined set of local actors.[12] The foremost concern on the interveners' side was how to overcome resistance and ensure local buy-in for their enterprise by engaging the 'right' local constituencies rather than taking issue directly and systematically with the latter's concerns.[13]

---

[7]Simon Chesterman, 'Ownership in Theory And In Practice: Transfer of Authority in UN Statebuilding Operations', *Journal of Intervention and Statebuilding*, 1, no. 1 (2007): 3–26.
Daniel Bendix and Ruth Stanley, 'Deconstructing Local Ownership of Security Sector Reform: A Review of the Literature', *African Security Review* 17, no. 2 (2008): 93–104.

[8]Timothy Donais, 'Dayton +20: Peacebuilding and the Perils of Exlusivity', *Peacebuilding* 5, no. 1 (2017): 7–21. See also a paper in this volume by Véronique Dudouet, Alia Ashaq, Ekaterine Basilaia and Nani Macharashvili, From policy to action: Assessing the European Union's approach to inclusive mediation and dialogue support in Georgia and Yemen.

[9]Bodille Arensman, Margit van Wessel and Dorothea Hilhorst, 'Does Local Ownership Bring about Effectiveness? The Case of Transnational Advocacy Networks', *Third World Quarterly* 38, no 6. (2017): 1311.

[10]Vesna Bojicic-Dzelilovic, Denisa Kostovicova and David Rampton, 'Statebuilding, Nationbuilding and Reconstruction', in *The Handbook of Global Security Policy*, eds. Mary Kaldor and Iavor Rangelov (Cambridge: Polity Press,2014), 265–82.

[11]In practice, local ownership is understood in different ways by local and international actors. See: Beatrice Pouligny, *Supporting Local Ownership in Humanitarian Action* (Berlin: Global Policy Institute, 2009); and Paula Pickering, *Peacebuilding in the Balkans: The View from the Ground Floor* (Ithaca: Cornell University Press, 2007).

[12]de Coning, 'Understanding Peacebuilding as Essentially Local'; and Does, *Inclusivity and Local Perspectives*.

[13]Ursula C. Schroeder and Fairlie Chappuis, 'New Perspectives on Security Sector Reform: The Role of Local Agency and Domestic Politics', *International Peacekeeping* 21, no. 2 (2014): 133–48; Volke Boege, Patricia Rinck and Tobias Debiel, Local- International Relations and the Recalibration of Peacebuilding Interventions: Insights from the 'Laboratory' of Bougainville and Beyond, NEF Report 112/2017 (Essen: University of Duisburg Essen, 2017).

This phase of local ownership scholarship was criticised for its focus on external interveners,[14] as deficient in its account of 'the local' component of peacebuilding, and by extension local ownership. The charge was that inadequate conceptualisation of the local resulted in a lack of ontological relevance of local ownership in practice and intractable problems in translating the conceptualisation of the local into programming concepts.[15] The ensuing scholarship of the so-called local turn reconceptualised the local to capture its plural, fluid, dynamic and agential quality – in other words to identify the 'true' local – and proposed to put the local as everyday practice at the centre of peacebuilding practice.[16] Instead of relying on pre-defined prescriptive frameworks and the local as given, from this perspective, external interveners and scholars are invited to engage contextually with the local forms of agency and their unexpected capacities.[17] The most notable practice response was a change in the approach to inclusion that extended outreach to 'atypical' local interlocutors including prominently women and youth as well as other traditionally marginalised categories, notably internally displaced population and minority groups. Another practice change was more systematic engagement of civil society organisations in preparations and evaluations of strategic documents evident in the UN, the EU and other major actors engaged in peacebuilding and conflict prevention. This still myopic interpretation of inclusivity in practice echoed a criticism some scholars expressed that the local turn perspective engaged insufficiently with local agency and that this in turn generated another set of practice problems.[18] As a result, peacebuilding practice continued to be poorly equipped to deliver on the normative promise of local ownership.[19]

The source of this enduring difficulty to operationalise local ownership is ultimately a cognitive one. While the first phase of local ownership scholarship highlighted the problems of insufficient agency, local turn scholars go further in viewing agency as not only a premise of locally owned peacebuilding but also a challenge to the international community's liberal peace project. Both phases see local agency in terms of resistance, but on different grounds. In the early local ownership debates, resistance was about a misfit between the external and local understanding of peace;

[14]Richmond, 'Beyond Local Ownership', 1311; Arensman, van Wessel and Hilhorst, 'Does Local Ownership Bring about Effectiveness?'.

[15]Lauren Hutton, *South Sudan: From Fragility at Independence to a Crisis of Sovereignity* (The Hague: Clingendael Netherlands Institute of International Relations, 2014), 9.

[16]Oliver Richmond and Jason Franks, 'Liberal Hubris? Virtual Peace in Cambodia', *Security Dialogue* 38, no. 1 (2007): 27–48; Caroline Hughes, Joakim Öjendal and Isabell Schierenbeck, 'The Struggle versus the Song', 82; Elisa Randazzo, 'The Paradox of the "Everyday": Scrutinising the Local Turn in Peacebuilding', *Third World Quarterly* 37, no. 8 (2016): 1351–70.

[17]Stefanie Kappler and Oliver Richmond, 'Peacebuilding and Culture in Bosnia and Herzegovina: Resistance or Emancipation?', *Security Dialogue* 42, no. 3 (2011): 274; and Joakim Öjendal and Sivhouch Ou, 'The "Local Turn" Saving Liberal Peacebuilding? Unpacking Virtual peace in Cambodia', *Third World Quarterly* 36, no. 5 (2015): 23.

[18]Andreas T. Hirblinger and Claudia Simons, 'The Good, the Bed, and the Powerful: Representations of the Local in Peacebuilding', *Security Dialogue* 46, no. 2 (2015): 422–39; Landon E. Hancock, 'Agency & Peacebuilding: The Promise of Local Zones of Peace', *Peacebuilding* 5, no. 3 (2017): 255–69; Tania Paffenholz, 'Unlocking the Local Turn in Peacebuilding: A Critical Assessment Towards and Agenda for Future Research', *Third World Quarterly* 36, no. 5 (2015): 857–74; Pickering, 'Peacebuilding in the Balkans'; Graeme William Young, 'Conceptualizing Resistance in Post-Conflict Environment', *International Peacekeeping* 22, no. 2 (2015): 169–85; and Jerry McCann, 'Local Ownership- An Imperative for Inclusive Peacebuilding', *Development Dialogue* (2015): 16–27.

[19]Isabell Schierenbeck, 'Beyond the Local Turn Divide: Lessons Learnt, Relearnt and Unlearnt', *Third World Quarterly 36*, no. 6 (2016): 1023–32; and Hirblinger and Simmons, 'The Good, the Bed and the Powerful'.

in the more recent accounts, the emphasis is on 'resistant agency'[20] whereby resistance is imbued with emancipatory potential. This assumption of local agency as either a deficit or a problem to overcome[21] has been tackled by a more recent process-centred, relational perspective on peacebuilding and local ownership, which foregrounds interactions, processes and practices in the local peacebuilding context.[22] Of particular note is the emphasis on pragmatism which 'directs attention to the everyday practices, strategies and institutions as a basis for addressing concrete problems at hand'[23] and the importance of 'how practices work in a particular context'.[24] In contrast to the rather abstract tenor of much of the scholarship on local ownership, a focus on relations and processes is seen as way to 'reach out into the everyday and pragmatically support local practices in addressing context specific challenges'.[25]

The notion of WOS offers one way of approaching the existing practices and processes of peacebuilding as a starting point to arrive at more constructive, peace-inducing relationships among the plethora of actors and agencies in the conflict space. It is a pragmatic and positivist – in a sense of objective and fact based – take on local agency as enacted through interactions of actors and process in a conflict space. A WOS approach suggests that intervention practice can acknowledge and reflect local responses to conflicts not only by attempting to engage with a greater diversity of local stakeholders but also through identifying combinations of significant non-state actors, taking account of relationships and interactions among local groups, and by recognising the breadth, depth and relevance of indigenous practices. This is to think about not only who constitutes local society but also how social actors exercise agency both individually, in conjunction with other locals and with internationals. Going further, the explicitly normative aspect of a WOS approach sees the presence of external intervention itself as a creative site of local conflict responses, providing additional dynamism and also glue for interactions at the grass roots, capturing elements of pragmatic engagement which are currently obscured. The shift in practice implied is to move away from a problematic view of local ownership and the local as something to be overcome and transformed, to recognising the resources inherent in how local actors respond to multiple security needs. It is also about crafting a capability out of recognising and building on the strategies they use to respond to the interconnected nature of vulnerabilities in the conflict space. Working with all these elements of inclusivity, the importance of relationships and the relevance of local practice responses to conflict, WOS seeks to shift policy mechanisms away from a dominant focus on elite bargains, programmatic

---

[20]Erin McCandless, Eric Abitbol and Timothy Donais, 'Vertical Integration: A Dynamic Practice Promoting Transformative Peacebuilding', *Journal of Peacebuilding and Development* 1, no. 3 (2015): 1–9.

[21]Schroeder and Chappuis,' New Perspectives on Security Sector Reform', 137.

[22]Wren, Chadwick, Tobias Debiel and Frank Gadinger, eds., *Relational Sensibility and 'The Turn to the Local: Prospects for the Future of Peacebuilding* (Duisburg: Centre for Global Cooperation Research, 2013).

[23]Louise Wiuff Moe, 'Relationality and Pragmatism in Peacebuilding: Reflections on Somaliland', in *Relational Sensibility and 'The Turn to the Local: Prospects for the Future of Peacebuilding*, eds. Wren, Chadwick, Tobias Debiel and Frank Gadinger (Duisburg: Centre for Global Cooperation Research, 2013), 46.

[24]David Chandler, 'Resilience and the "Everyday": Beyond the Paradox of Liberal Peace', *Review of International Studies* 41, no. 1(2015): 27–48.

[25]Chandler, 'Resilience and the "Everyday".'

interventions or capacity and institution building towards supporting and leveraging patterns of actorness and organisation in a local space.

In the following sections, we examine examples of local ownership in peacebuilding practice applying WOS as a prism which highlights three aspects: how inclusivity is pursued (both in terms of actors and processes), what kinds of relations are mobilised and what kinds of practices and processes local actors engage in to deal with multiple vulnerabilities of the conflict-affected population. We identify two particular social groups, namely private sector and faith groups, which merit investigation as neglected sites of local agency and provide lens for tracing different aspects of local ownership in practice.

Inclusivity

A tendency in external peacebuilding to focus on and privilege a relatively narrow group of locals, which can be characterised as government and non-government elites, is also characteristic of EU practices. There are many reasons for this, to do with process and conceptual issues that can lead to marginalisation of constituencies which may be integral to constructing a representative picture of local society and sites of agency and that are relevant in terms of building social capital of intervention. Sometimes, important constituencies are invisible and bypassed because, as Mac Ginty suggests, the internationals are simply not equipped to see the local[26], or because of physical and conflict geography of the locality, or because of the rules and regulations international actors follow in engaging with local constituencies such as funding priorities and procedures which delimit target beneficiaries to those who are able to apply for and implement external donor programmes, or excluding certain actors on ethical grounds.

We identified two types of groups in particular, namely private companies and faith groups which are under-acknowledged by external interventions. Yet, they are significant in terms of representing an important aspect of agency in the conflict space, either through their own identities and efforts within local society and/or their abilities to mobilise other social groups. Their marginalisation (while not being acknowledged within a category of 'marginalised' actors as typically understood in the mainstream peacebuilding theory and practice) illustrates persistent gaps in peacebuilding practice that operates on an implicit rationale of 'sufficient and inclusive enough'[27] engagement with local actors. This limited horizon of vision[28] undermines the effectiveness of intervention and stymies more substantial and dynamic forms of interaction between locals and internationals. In this sense, our focus on these two particular groups is

[26]Roger MacGinty, 'What Do We Mean When We Use the Term "Local"? Imagining and Framing the Local and International in Relation to Peace and Order', in *Peacebuilding in Crisis. Rethinking Paradigms and Practices of Transnational Cooperation*, eds. Tobias Diebel, Thomas Held and Ulrich Schnecker (London: Routledge 2016), 193–209.

[27]Does, *Inclusivity and Local Perspectives*.
According to Paffenholz, the reviews of two decades of peacebuilding show no genuine advance towards meaningful inclusion. Tania Paffenholz, 'International Peacebuilding Goes Local: Analysing Lederach's Conflict Transformation Theory and its Ambivalent Encounter with 20 Years of Practice', *Peacebuilding* 2, no. 1 (2014): 14.

[28]In Ukraine context, the case of internally displaced people joining the groups of activist working with war-affected population illustrate the external actors' misconception that the internally displaced are simply helpless victims of conflict.

illustrative of the gaps and missed opportunities for external peacebuilders to engage both vertically and horizontally with local society.

The private sector

The private sector is on the whole disconnected from mainstream peacebuilding interventions and its contribution is conceived as an indirect one through its role as a driver of economic growth and a provider of jobs. The private sector is however uniquely embedded in local society, with links across multiple societal levels that can be harnessed for peacebuilding goals or equally whose tendency to pursue particularistic interests needs to be addressed to prevent them undermining peace.[29] Companies are often primary providers of security in contexts where there is an absence of government or international governance. Examples of this include Yemen where the only international representatives on the ground after the Arab Spring were the security officials from oil companies; or in Ukraine where companies have continued operating in the territories controlled by separatists from which government and many civil society actors have withdrawn.[30]

Highlighting the multiple identities of the private sector which are shaped by the locally contingent social processes of conflict and deep social transformation unfolding in Ukraine are new forms of private sector activism geared towards governance reforms and broader socio-economic development objectives. The conflict that at the level of official politics and diplomacy is couched in terms of separatist movements and Russian occupation is internally also about transforming the economic and political model based on the rule of powerful oligarchs. Businessmen were among the leading figures of the Maidan 'revolution'[31] that predated the conflict; hence, possessing a dual identity as both commercial and social/political actors embedded in dense social networks. The European Business Association Ukraine[32] has taken up to improve governance standards and to counter corruption, as part of a broad agenda of national renewal outlined in the New Vision Statement, which emerged in response to the Maidan citizens' mobilisation. Formally separated into two opposing political camps – one under the formal jurisdiction of the Ukraine government, the other belonging to the separatist government – business on both sides of the divide shares a concern over rising criminality which is a consequence of disruption to the legal economy. Rising criminality which deforms Ukraine's economic and social fabric as well as compounds everyday insecurity is a problem with potential for long-lasting consequences on governance and economic development. However, its pernicious impact on the everyday life of Ukraine's communities has been largely ignored by the political elites and its

[29]Brian Ganson and Achim Wennmann, *Business and Conflict in Fragile States: The Case for Pragmatic Solutions* (London: Routledge 2016); and Nicke Killick, VS Srikantha and Canan Gűnduz, *The Role of Local Business in Peacebuilding* (Berlin: Berghof Foundation, 2005).

[30]Hubert de Bremond, Total – Civil Society Dialogue Network (presentation, *'Private Sector and Conflict'* 29 October 2012, Brussels).

[31]Maidan 'revolution' refers to mass gathering of citizens at Kiev's Maidan square in February 2014 at the height of the Orange Revolution to democratise Ukraine.

[32]Interview with Oleksii Chiuev, 8 September 2016, Kiev. Interview with Oleksandra Romancova 7 September 2016, Kiev. After the Maidan events, around 2000 businessmen worked together on a document Vision New Ukraine that sets a comprehensive reform agenda for the country. Businessmen also take up voluntary work with the non-governmental organisations.

international interlocutors focused on finding political solution to the conflict.[33] At the same time, the private sector's awareness of and responsiveness to the immediate needs of the conflict-affected population in Ukraine are manifested in their proactive role in securing employment for internally displaced people with women and older workers as priority categories by using a government tax facilitation scheme.[34]

Faith groups

Among scholars and peacebuilding practitioners, religion tends to be framed predominantly in terms of a conflict driver, rather than treating religious groups as a category of socio-political actor with peacebuilding potential.[35] Their comparative advantage associated with long-term presence and commitment and their spiritual and moral authority, often combined with economic resources, are insufficiently acknowledged in peacebuilding practice. Experience of peacebuilding shows many examples where faith groups have assumed a public profile in formal (and informal) processes of multitrack diplomacy and somewhat less so in other policy areas such as SSR and governance reform. The civil authority of faith groups has been successfully leveraged in processes of reconciliation, access to justice and conflict mediation as illustrated by the role of the local religious groups in Mozambique, Sudan and Uganda.[36]

In Ukraine and Georgia, the involvement of the Moscow Patriarchate of the Orthodox Church in political debates and the behaviour of church officials in disputed territories have contributed to defining the external analysis of those conflicts, whereas the church's ongoing everyday responses to the conflicts are also interesting in revealing its role in peacebuilding and conflict prevention.[37] In Ukraine, the Russian Orthodox Church is an influential socio-economic actor with an economic portfolio in agriculture, tourism, and construction as well as a provider of education; it also has a stake in over 400 print and electronic media which affords it multiple channels of influence in local society.[38]

As well as an ambiguous political actor, at another level of action, the Russian Orthodox Church has supported the work of volunteer brigades consisting of churchgoers and civil society organisations in providing humanitarian assistance in Eastern Ukraine and psychosocial care for internally displaced people. The brigades also provide practical advice on relocation, employment opportunities and other needs of displaced population. 'Save Ukraine' is a fusion of religious and secular groups that operate a brigade style system in providing humanitarian aid in 24 locations across the

[33]Interview with Vadym Fomin, 8 September 2016 Kiev.

[34]Interview with the staff of the employment centre for internally displaced people, 9 September 2016, Kiev. Interview with Sergeiy Solodkyy, 9 September 2016 Kiev.

[35]Katrien Hertog, *Complex Reality of Religious Peacebuilding: The Conceptual Contributions and Critical Analysis* (New York: Rowman and Littlefield Publishers, 2010); and Harold Coward and Gordon S. Smith, eds. *Religion and Peacebuilding* (Albany: State University of New York Press, 2004).

[36]Joshua Haynes, 'Conflict, Conflict Resolution and Peace-building: The Role of Religion in Mozambique, Nigeria and Cambodia', *Commonwealth and Comparative Politics* 47, no. 1 (2009): 52–75; and Tjesard Bouta, S. Ayse Kadayifci-Orellana and Mohammed Abu-Nimer, *Faith-based Peace-building: Mapping and Analysis of Christian, Muslim and Multi-faith Actors* (The Hague: Clingendael Netherlands Institute of International Relations, 2005).

[37]Serhiy Zdioruk and Olexiy Haran, 'The Russian Orthodox Church as an Instrument of Russia's Foreign Policy towards Ukraine', in *Religion as the Instrument of Russian Foreign Policy towards Neighbouring Countries Georgia, Latvia, Ukraine*, ed. Tengiz Pkhaldze (Tbilisi: *International Centre for Geopolitical Studies 2012), 54–101.*

[38]Zdiouruk and Haran 'The Russian Orthodox Church', 60.

borderline between government and separatist territories; they also provide moral and spiritual support to internally displaced and former fighters; it also runs a hot line for any citizens needing advice and help.[39]

From a WOS perspective, besides reaching out to 'hidden' and overlooked actors, the process of inclusion itself is consequential in ensuring more locally relevant peacebuilding by supporting existing capabilities and resources. Gaining ground in the development aid community, and much less so among peacebuilding practitioners despite theoretical advances pointing in that direction, is an approach of 'locally led' initiatives intended to tap into latent local capabilities.[40] By way of illustration, in Kenya, the Danish government development agency supported a combination of religious-based and development organisations, some of which were informal groups of volunteers, to work on conflict resolution and terrorism prevention so that they were able to define the priorities and main lines of actions. Such an approach enables those organisations to engage with a range of actors including armed youth, religious preachers and terror suspects whose participation in conflict prevention and peacebuilding is fundamentally important and yet sidelined in official peacebuilding and conflict prevention practices of the EU and most key international players.[41] Here, the different qualities of faith groups, in particular their moral and spiritual authority in some contexts, that allow them to mobilise for peace often the most unlikely of social groups are important and yet underutilised aspect of local agency.

A relational perspective

For peacebuilding practice, one of the most pertinent issues around local ownership is identifying 'the right' interlocutors within a host society who could take on board peacebuilding and preventing the 'wrong' type of actors from being empowered.[42] Such a simplistic understanding downplays the local complexities associated with a plurality of actors, actors' multiple identities and the dynamic aspects of agency due to continuously changing interests, motives and priorities of those actors. In reality, aggregated groupings such as confessional associations, and even more the private sector, are diverse in nature and harbour different agendas. This diversity within 'black boxes' of corporate actors implies opportunities for multiplier effects, as individual organisations' agendas coincide and cross other interests in society, including other companies, and alternative religious affiliations. Both the potential and the pitfalls of such diversity can be neglected by a tunnel view towards local actors which overlooks their composite identity and dynamic relationships among different actor groups.

A different approach has been tried in Colombia, where peacebuilders attempted to capture the versatile role of the private sector at the subnational level through the Peace Laboratories project which encouraged various forms of partnering with other social actors, namely local government officials, civil society and the church in a grass-root initiative that addressed multidimensional insecurities in Colombian regions. The Colombian government has historically had an uneven territorial presence and such

[39]Interview with Igor Nebava, Save Ukraine, 7 September 2016, Kiev.
[40]Rosie Pinnington, '*Local First in Practice: Unlocking the Power to Get Things Done* (London: Peace Direct, 2014).
[41]Pinnington, 'Local First in Practice', 32.
[42]ibid., 26.

grass-root initiatives that mobilise local capacities throughout society are of vital importance for the prospect of so-called territorial peace. Such 'partnerships' challenge the idea of the unitary state which informs the approach to local ownership in peacebuilding practice in favour of working with different components of Colombian society and their indigenous forms and drawing on synergy between secular and religious peacebuilding processes.

In Ukraine, the ability of the European Business Association to draw on support from diaspora is an example of how a diverse geography of peacebuilding and diverse relationships are being mobilised and deployed to create new sites of activism and authority. In responding to conflict developments on the ground, the association has expanded its international contacts and collaboration in order to strengthen its standing with the government and establish its credibility as a peacebuilding actor. The association has taken advantage of the EU presence to secure EU backing to increase its own international profile. This emboldened status is seen as a step towards the association eventually getting a seat at the table to formally participate in the dialogue with the government over the future peace settlement.[43] Simultaneously, at a different level of interaction, companies in Ukraine, some of which are the members of the association – particularly in Kiev which has a large internally displaced population – have been actively involved in tripartite relations with the government, civil society organisations and volunteer groups in supporting aforementioned work placement schemes for the internally displaced population.[44]

As regards faith groups, the comparative advantage of religious leaders has been noted in conducting conflict mediation by working in concert with a range of other stakeholders constituting a form of relational asset which offers the chance to advance more integrative peacebuilding. Excluding faith groups from internationally sponsored dialogues, for example because of a locally declared government commitment to secularism, can have detrimental effects on the relationships among different groups in societies where spiritual and confessional orientations within the local population are significant.[45] One example of this kind of tension between the secular framing of international intervention and local practices is Somalia and Nigeria where the role of religious groups in peacebuilding over the secular channels has been particularly pronounced.[46] In Ukraine, the Orthodox-dominated Ukrainian Council of Churches is an established interlocutor of government but other faith groups including Catholic, Jewish, Muslim and Buddhist are denied representation in the Council.[47] As a result, the members of Ukraine's Army of Islamic faith are not provided with spiritual assistance, which closes a potentially creative channel of representation and communication while creating further grounds for social tensions.[48]

The significance of diverse groups being able to forge diverse types of relationships is illustrated by the aforementioned example of volunteer brigades in Ukraine, which originated in an initiative started by a cohort of churchgoers – initially only three –[49] who were able to leverage their personal relations on both sides of

[43]Interview with Oleksii Chiuev, 8 September 2016, Kiev.

[44]Interview with the staff of the employment centre for internally displaced people, 8 September 2016, Kiev.

[45]Douglas Johnston and Cynthia Sampson, Religion, *The Missing Dimension of* Statecraft (Oxford: Oxford University Press, 2004).

[46]Bouta, Kadayifci-Orellana and Abu-Nimer, Faith-based Peace-building.

[47]Interview with Said Ismagilov, Mufti of Ukraine, 8 September 2016, Kiev.

[48]ibid.

[49]Interview with Igor Nebava, 8 September 2016, Kiev.

Ukraine's conflict to organise and work collaboratively to assist local population according to their own assessment of needs and priorities. In this particular example, a potential for building diverse and multilevel relationships reflects the ability of faith groups to mobilise for peace beyond their own communities, and to work both in concert with as well as in parallel to other faith and secular groups, locally and transnationally, that remain insufficiently integrated with other peacebuilding efforts.

Complementary practices

Plural constituencies in the conflict space reflect not only different geographies and experiences but also imply a diversity of attitudes to the conflict, different expectations regarding outcomes and anticipated results of external intervention. As a result, there are multiple opportunities for conflict responses, and a range of peacebuilding activities both independent of and in conjunction with external actors which reflect local understanding of problems and community needs.

The issue of sequencing of civilian peacebuilding has been identified as a key policy and practice challenge to local ownership.[50] Locally organised groups of activists, whatever their motivation (for example religious or business), are particularly effective in providing bridging activities between humanitarian assistance at the sharp end of active conflict and underlying reforms to embed peace as well as between medium and longer term assistance. The ability of small local actors to implement transitional activities is illustrated by the case of 'Save Ukraine' group. Mobilised initially around humanitarian and emergency assistance, the group has established its credibility through access to constituencies with extreme human security needs through timely and local intervention. Subsequent activities and services were adapted through a proximate knowledge of next steps required which included for example livelihood strategies for the conflict-affected population that led to 'Save Ukraine' developing a programme to assist individuals with setting up bakery businesses.[51] This is an example of pragmatic sequencing of interventions, which illustrates how coordination of different actors and activities takes place on the ground as the peacebuilding process unfolds in contrast to pre-existing protocols and frameworks drawn by the interveners.[52] Furthermore, this example illustrates how such small, local indigenous forms of engagement and practices are able to respond to a range of problems from food insecurity, lack of livelihoods, lack of dignity and governance issues. In contrast, the interconnected nature of such multiple vulnerabilities facing conflict-affected populations is poorly addressed by operational practices characterised by silo mentality among different peacebuilding organisations along with poor adaptive[53] and coordination

[50]Alan Bryden, Timothy Donais and Heiner Hänggi, *Shaping a Security Governance Agenda in Post-Conflict Peacebuilding* (Geneva: Geneva Centre for the Democratic Control of Armed Forces (DCAF) Policy Paper, no. *11* November, 2005); and Adam Moore, *Peacebuilding in Practice. Local Experience in Two Bosnian Towns* (New York: Cornell University Press. 2013).

[51]Interview with Igor Nebava, 7 September 2016, Kiev.

[52]Moix, 'Choosing Peace'.

[53]Comparing the slow response of key international organisations involved in peacebuilding and conflict resolution in Ukraine with the flexibility and adaptability of the volunteers groups, the head of the umbrella organisation of volunteers described those organisations as 'tankers on the sea' in contrast with the nimbleness of the local activist groups. Interview with Igor Nebava, 7 September Kiev, 2016.

capabilities. A similar example of complementary local practices that approach peacebuilding and conflict resolution holistically is that of the Centre for Resolution of Conflicts in DRC which works on reintegration of demobilised soldiers, by relying on a large pool of volunteers who work across different policy areas and with different community groups to ensure peaceful reintegration and support social cohesion. This approach contrasts with fragmented process of reintegration in the context of institutionally focused DDR reforms.[54]

The fluid and highly connective nature of local activism not only shapes the universe of local counterparties, including the emergence of 'new' actors, it also has a bearing on the type of practices in the conflict space and different combinations of actors involved. In Ukraine, the volunteer phenomenon is not only present among religious groups but stems from civic engagement with the 2014 Maidan Euro-revolution, based on common feelings of national identity across multiple social groups. Technology and social media have provided the means of permanent and ongoing connections between different groups and increased the level of mobilisation within local society. This has facilitated the formation of ad hoc groupings and alliances of local actors, which shift according to circumstance and whose objectives are a complex mix of addressing the impact of conflict while working towards societal transformation. They have become a feature of the conflict landscape, responding in immediate ways, with not only quick response times but a high degree of adaptability which is an essential aspect from a local ownership perspective. The funding and strategic priorities of these groups tend to have a short life cycle, and this limits their possibilities to secure financial backing from large donors which cater to more established civil society organisations with capacity to administer large grants over longer period of time. Yet, these groups are better able to adapt to the rapid evolution of events on the ground and changing priorities and develop small and short term but nevertheless often vital projects which target specific groups; for example, older women, disabled former combatants or those traumatised by conflict and requiring psychological as well as practical help to re-enter the workforce. Local groups, such as the 'Save Ukraine' volunteers, are also more present in small towns and villages than international organisations typically focused on larger population centres, leading to a variable geography related to issues such as social justice, human rights and economic opportunities.

The issue of funding local counterparties in peacebuilding is often at the forefront of the scholarly debates and practical concerns including a risk of propping up the 'wrong local'. And yet in Ukraine, because of the specific context in which many types of civil organisations have emerged inspired by a national rejuvenation agenda, there are examples of local civil society organisations that have declined financial support from big donors, the EU included. The employment centre for internally displaced people in Kiev, established by a group of Maidan activists, as a Facebook page, and with initial financial support from the EU, took a view that the EU programme limited to Eastern Ukraine was not appropriate and that supporting internally displaced people throughout the country better reflected local priorities which led it to turn down the EU funding.[55] Instead, the centre asked the EU officials to publicly endorse its work which gives it more

[54]Kate McGuiness, ed., *Local First: Development for the Twenty-First Century* (London: Peace Direct, 2012.)
[55]Interview at the employment centre for internally displaced people, 8 September 2016 Kiev.

leverage in pressuring the government to participate in some of the centre's initiatives. The centre also took advantage of the USAID assistance in the form of free office space which it shares with three other indigenous organisations working on different areas of peacebuilding. Sharing premises has been conducive to collaboration among the four groups of activists in designing programmes that are more effective in responding to the impact of conflict and resulted in new opportunities for joint fundraising. Thus, here, the question is less about local ownership of international initiatives and more about how effectively external policies grasp dynamics on the ground, recognising diverse modalities of interactions among the international and local actors. This includes the fact that internationals are able to play both a direct (funding) and indirect role (in this case political support which improves the finance-raising abilities of local actors) in encouraging the diversity of local conflict responses that can be mutually beneficial.

Unofficial and ad hoc coalitions between different groups create entry points for external actors to penetrate remote locations and areas where access is difficult and communications fluctuate, either as a result of 'hot' conflict or because of cultural barriers around marginalised groups, and in this way, these entry points serve to complement activities that tend to be biased towards urban centres. In contemporary conflicts, where active conflict is confined to particular parts of the country, while the capital may be relatively stable, the physical and affective distance between external practitioners, with few field offices or outposts and nuclei of conflict, constitutes a gap in the possibility for more encompassing and mutually beneficial peacebuilding interactions. This makes activists an important and topical sounding board for international peacebuilders to test both the extent and depth of needs, achieve real time, bottom-up analysis of the conflict and its impacts and to develop appropriate responses. Religious groups in Crimea and Eastern Ukraine, which suffer persistent human rights harassment by the local Russian-backed authorities, have for example served as early warning posts for international peacebuilders of confrontation and for particular sites of social tension.

Particularly in cases where there are huge movements of population – such as in Georgia, Ukraine and Yemen as a result of the conflict – the challenges of engaging with rapidly changing demographics as well as being adaptable to a shifting reality on the ground are an important aspect of local ownership in practice, which determines the effectiveness of traditional interventions by the EU and other actors. For example, the task of holding elections in eastern Ukraine is hampered by the organisational problem of 70,000 unregistered voters and over 100,000 registered voters who in September 2016 when this research was conducted were on the Russian side of the border.

Conclusions

Rather than viewing local ownership in instrumental terms by one side to bring about greater engagement with and by local actors, we have sought to analyse local ownership as part of a capability to leverage positive social attributes of external-local (including local–local) relations in a context of conflict and post-conflict. Where existing practices of local ownership enact an imprecise combination of process and goal orientated strategies, this perspective led us to investigate the social relationships and connections within interventions as well as indigenous capacities for action in addition to simply focusing on which groups are engaged by externals, and the modes for encouraging their involvement. From this starting point, a

WOS approach offers an analytical view of local ownership, not as an instrumental process of mitigating negative perceptions of intervention, or reifying the local, or for that matter another version of a bottom-up peacebuilding. Foremost, it sees local ownership in terms of developing a new capacity. The combination of horizontal and vertical axes introduced in the introduction to this collection of papers to capture multilevel, multiactor dynamics (vertical axis) and processes and practices across different fields of peacebuilding action (horizontal axis) offers an operational perspective based on leveraging the density and complexity of conflict responses. This includes those responses which are generated at subnational levels often in informal ways and in geographies traditionally unmarked by conventional peacebuilding through multilevel processes of interactions characterising conflict space. As such, WOS perspective on local ownership addresses two criticisms of the local ownership in peacebuilding which concern the identification of the local and the local/international dichotomy. As a practice perspective, it serves to enhance inclusivity as well as to make visible relational dynamics and reveal a process dimension to the local which incorporates agency but also indigenous customs, cultures and responses to conflict which offer constructive entry points for engagement by external peacebuilders. Taken together, these additional elements of a WOS approach explained in the introductory article to this collection of papers constitute a thicker dialogue between interveners and local populations which can inject new meaning and clarity to the norm of local ownership.

Disclosure statement

No potential conflict of interest was reported by the authors.

Funding

The research for the article was conducted as part of the project Whole of Society Conflict Prevention and Peacebuilding (WOSCAP), funded by the EU's Horizon 2020 Research and Innovation Programme: [Grant agreement number 653866].

Bracing the wind and riding the norm life cycle: inclusive peacebuilding in the European capacity building mission in Sahel–Mali (EUCAP Sahel–Mali)

Shyamika Jayasundara-Smits

ABSTRACT

Since the political crisis in 2012, the European Union has stepped up its commitment to Mali and the Sahel using various external intervention instruments gathered under the Common Security and Defence Policy (CSDP). These instruments are designed to achieve functional and normative goals of the EU. Situating in the debate on normative actorness of the EU and by applying the Whole-of-Society (WOS) approach to conflict prevention and peacebuilding, this paper investigates how the European Capacity Building mission for the Malian Security Forces (EUCAP Sahel–Mali) is operationalising two key EU-SSR-related norms – local ownership and inclusivity– and manoeuvres context and programme specific challenges. By analysing the mission-training/capacity building and outreach, this paper argues the EUCAP mission has been largely functional than normative driven, thus reducing the EU's overall reputation as a normative actor, particularly in the area of security. This paper offers practical recommendations to reach the EU's normative goals via SSR.

Introduction

Situated in the ongoing debates on norms[1] in international politics and external intervention, this paper investigates the EU's normative actorness,[2] in the fields of conflict prevention and peacebuilding, and in particular, the contribution to Security Sector Reform (SSR) as a discreet field of normative action.[3] With the

[1]Norms are defined as ideas of varying degrees of abstraction and specification with respect to fundamental values, organising principles or standardised procedures that resonate across many states and global actors, having gained support in multiple forums including official policies, laws, treaties or agreements. Norms are also understood as standards of behaviour based on inter-subjective validity. L.Zimmerman, *Global Norms with a Local Face: Rule-of-Law Promotion and Norm Translation* (Cambridge: Cambridge University press 2017):7.

[2]H.Bull,'Civilian Power Europe: A Contradiction in Terms?'. *JCMS: Journal of Common Market Studies*, 21, no2 (1982):149–170; I. Manners, ' Normative Power Europe: A Contradiction in Terms?'. JCMS: *Journal of Common Market Studies*, 40 (2002): 235–258.

[3]E.Gordon, A.C.Welch and E.Roos, 'Security Sector Reform and the Paradoxical Tension between Local Ownership and Gender Equality'. *Stability: International Journal of Security and Development*, 4, no.1), (2015):53. T. A. Donais, ' Inclusion or Exclusion? Local Ownership and Security Sector Reform', *Studies in Social Justice*', 3, no. 1 (2009): 117–131. A.J.Bellamy, 'Security Sector Reform: Prospects and Problems', *Peace, Security & Global Change* (formerly Pacifica Review) 15, no.2 (2003): 101–119. P. Jackson, 'Security Sector Reform and State Building', *Third World Quarterly* 32, no.10 (2011): 1803–1822. R.Kunz, 'Gender and

return of realpolitik and the realist security dilemma in international politics and the move by the EU to define its overall approach to security and foreign affairs based on 'principled-pragmatism',[4] the EU has come under increased critical scrutiny regarding the delivery of its normative commitments.

Despite the commitment to combine principles/norms with pragmatism, scholars observe that pragmatism is increasingly taking precedence over principles and norms.[5] In the case of SSR, the imbalance between the functional and normative imperative of EU actions can be partly explained owing to the contextually rooted challenges met by SSR missions in third countries. However, a more robust inquiry based on a flexible yet analytically rich framework is needed to capture the other challenges experienced by the EU, especially the ones that are programme specific and the challenges emanating from a process of dynamic interactions between the context and programme goals.

Whole-of-Society approach (WOS)[6]

The paper uses the 'Whole-of-Society' (WOS) approach to conflict prevention and peacebuilding to propose that the EU could enhance the normative dimension of its SSR interventions, compared to the principled pragmatism approach, through a clearer focus on the normative standards such as inclusivity, ownership and gender equality, which are implied but which appear to have been eclipsed or relegated in recent examples of SSR missions such as EUCAP Sahel.

The WOS approach is both a prescriptive and a normative ideal. As a prescriptive approach, 'WOS' assumes that peacebuilding and conflict prevention will be more effective when a broad(er) range of actions and intentions are identified and taken into account. As a normative approach, WOS emphasises the importance of inclusivity as a key principle of external interventions. In this sense, the term 'WOS' refers to ambitions which underpinned and motivated the Mali SSR intervention. The paper seeks to critically assess the range of actors with which the EU engaged and identify related issues of exclusion and marginalisation as part of the engagement process. By focusing on presences–absences, inclusions–exclusions and the marginalisation–elevation of certain actors over the others, we hope to show the opportunities for enhancing these normative aspects of the EUCAP Sahel–Mali mission, as well as the implications for not so doing.

In this paper, we refer to 'inclusivity' to denote both actors and spaces in a conflict environment. It refers to the degree of access to meaningful participation and decision-making by a range of actors concerned with/affected by a given conflict, beyond the most powerful elites. These actors can vary from community-based organisations to ordinary citizens to the potential spoilers, who can exercise meaningful voice and

---

Security Sector Reform: Gendering Differently?', *International Peacekeeping* 21, no.5(2014): 604–622. M.Sedra, 'The Hollowing-Out of the Liberal Peace Project in Afghanistan: The Case of Security Sector Reform', *Central Asian Survey* 32, no.3(2013): 371–387.

[4]EU External Action Service (EEAS GSFSP), 'Shared Vision, Common Action: A Stronger Europe – A Global Strategy for the European Union's Foreign and Security Policy'. Brussels (2016)..

[5]S.Biscop, 'The EU Global Strategy: Realpolitik with European Characteristics' in Might and Right in World Politics, International Security: a European – South American Dialogue 2016, Konrad-Adenauer-Stiftung, Rio de Janeiro (2016).

[6]This section of the article is built on M.Martin, V.Bojicic-Dzelilovic, C. van der Borgh and G. Frerks' WOSCAP theoretical and Methodological Framework', London School of Economics and Political Science, Utrecht University (2015).

agency in the design and the implementation of SSR.[7] We assume being inclusive will minimise resistance and rejection from the often marginalised yet vocal/hardliner actors and increase legitimacy and responsibility of the programme and of its outcomes from a wide range of constituencies with the ability to exercise voice and protect their interests throughout the reform process. Overall, by applying the WOS approach to the EUCAP Sahel mission we hope to show how the EU could identify and address some of the challenges related to norm operationalising, diffusion and internalisation via SSR both at vertical and horizontal levels. In the WOS framework, vertical axis represents an actor perspective with a focus on normative and practical/operational challenges to improve inclusivity and engage a wide range of actors in peacebuilding interventions. The horizontal axis comprises multiple actions located in different fields of practice and policy.[8] By doing so, we hope to highlight some problem-solving possibilities within the mission and offer suggestions how a WOS approach could assist the EU to adapt and reform SSR practices in the future.

In the following section, we present the normative trajectory of the EU-SSR, then the key objectives of the EUCAP Sahel–Mali mission, highlighting the functional and the normative agendas underpinning them. Next, the paper analyses how key SSR norms- local ownership and inclusivity (including gender) have been operationalised in the EUCAP Sahel mission and the challenges in doing so. In the concluding section, the paper offers practical suggestions on what the EU could do to overcome some of the challenges identified for norm realisation, through applying a WOS perspective.

The normative trajectory of the EU-SSR

SSR is an indispensable element of the EU's combined approach to state building, conflict prevention and peacebuilding. Drawing from the OECD definition[9] the EU defines SSR as

> the process of transforming a country's security system, so that it gradually provides individuals and the state with more effective and accountable security in a manner consistent with respect for human rights, democracy, the rule of law and the principles of good governance. SSR is a long-term and political process, as it goes to the heart of power relations in a country. It needs to be nationally driven and requires political commitment and leadership, inter-institutional cooperation and broad stakeholder participation to achieve the widest possible consensus.

Although a clear definition of SSR is a relatively recent development in EU policy, since the early 1990s, the EU has undertaken many SSR-related activities.[10] The present form and the content of EU-SSR is the outcome of a complex interplay between various norms, ideas, interests and the contestation and negotiation

[7]T.Donais and E.McCandless,' International Peace Building and the Emerging Inclusivity Norm', *Third World Quarterly*, 38, no.2 (2017):293.

[8]Refer to the introductory article of this volume for an elaborate discussion of these two axes.

[9]OECD. The OECD DAC Handbook on Security System Reform: supporting security and justice OECD, Paris, at: www.oecd.org/dataoecd/43/25/38406485.pdf. (2007):5.

[10]F. Longo, 'Externalization of the Internal Security Strategy in the Framework of Multilateralism: The Case of Security Sector Reform', in *New Challenges for the EU Internal Security Strategy*, eds. Maria O'Neill, Ken Swinton, Aaron Winter (Cambridge Scholars Publishing, (2013):244.

between knowledge and power among the above mentioned three epistemic communities.[11] Since the Feira Council meeting (2000) that established SSR as an important goal of the EU's external policy, SSR is being regularly featured as one of EU's flagship programme. In the backdrop of changing geo-strategic relations and the looming 'conventional security dilemma',[12] today SSR has even become a strategic priority.[13] Furthermore, SSR can be regarded as a testing ground and a measure of EU's normative actorness. However, both the normative and functional achievements of the EU-SSR are not without criticisms. One main and recurrent criticism is SSR being the linchpin of EU's liberal state building and peacebuilding project.[14] For the EU, SSR is very much a technical as well as a political process. While the technical underscores the functional imperative, the political underscores the normative .[15] Thus, via SSR, the EU strives to assist third countries to be effective in their security provisioning by balancing the state's monopoly of violence and monopoly of legitimacy.[16] Monopoly of legitimacy is primarily sought by applying a plethora of liberal normative principles: human rights, democracy, and rule of law, good governance, local ownership, human security, inclusivity and gender equality.

Since its origins, the EU has been perceived as a norm entrepreneur/inventor and diffuser,[17] due to its explicit normative commitments. [18] The EU's normative actorness hinges on its ability to effectively and sustainably diffuse as well as help internalise EU's norms through interventions in a third country, and in this respect the EU has struggled sometimes due to zero-adoption, selective adoption and resistance it has encountered. Moreover the EU's track record of implementing and realising these norms in a third country via SSR is rather poor.[19] As

[11]G. Faleg, 'Between Knowledge and Power: Epistemic Communities and the Emergence of Security Sector Reform in the EU Security Architecture', *European Security*, 21, no2, (2012):167. Epistemic community as a network of professionals from a variety of disciplines and backgrounds, who share a common set of normative and principled beliefs which guide their social actions, having a shared causal beliefs based on their analysis of practices and a shared notions of validity characterised by intersubjective, internally defined criteria for weighing and validating knowledge and a common policy enterprise. P.M.Haas, Introduction: Epistemic Communities and International Policy Coordination', *International Organization, Knowledge, Power, and International Policy Coordination*, 46, no. 1 (19,920):3.

[12]Refers to a situation in which actions taken by a state to increase its own security (usually by military means) cause reactions from other states, which in turn lead to a decrease rather than an increase in the original state's security in J.Herz, *Political Realism and Political Idealism: A Study in Theories and Realities*, (Chicago: University of Chicago Press 1951).

[13]The EU Global Strategy – Year 1 at: https://europa.eu/globalstrategy/en/vision-action.

[14]T. A. Donais, 'Empowerment or Imposition? Dilemmas of Local Ownership in Post-Conflict Peacebuilding Processes', *Peace & Change*, 34, no. 1 (2009):6.

[15]Here, the functional imperative refers to the ability to deploy force against external threats, efficiently and effectively. In other words 'get the job done'. The normative imperative which is also understood as societal imperative. This is equivalent to soft power. In the case of EU-SSR, this is derived from the European Liberal values and institutions. In previous research the scholars have explored the tension between these two imperatives, where optimising functional imperative is affected by normative imperative. S.Jayasundara-Smits, 'Civil-Military Synergy at Operational Level in EU External Action', Global Partnership for the Prevention of Armed Conflict (GPPAC), The Hague (2016):8.

[16]S.Jayasundara-Smits and L.Schirch, 'EU and Security Sector Reform: Tilting at Windmills?' WOSCAP-EU, Global Partnership for the Prevention of Armed Conflict (GPPAC), The Hague (2015):3.

[17]See L.Zimmermann, 'Same, Same or Different? Norm Diffusion Between Resistance, Compliance, and Localization in Post-conflict States', International Studies Perspectives, 1–19 (2014):100.

This distinction of stages is derived from the 'norm life-cycle' model of Finnemore and Sikkink 1998. In the norm diffusion literature, specific local context in which a norms are promoted and the different outcomes of norm diffusion: resistance, full adoption, or a decoupling of rules and practices is captured.

[18]K.Vadura,'The EU as 'Norm Entrepreneur' in the Asian Region: Exploring the Digital Diplomacy Aspect of the Human Rights Toolbox', *Asia Europe Journal*, 13, no.3, (2015):349–360.

conventional wisdom of SSR research points out, deviating from a genuine bottom–up community centric approach (over the state centric approach) is one example of this. Deviating from the bottom–up approach means inviting room for rejection, disrespect, co-optation and marginalisation or even manipulation of the security needs of the (marginalised) communities by the powerful local actors. Instead, norm hybridisation is a notable outcome of SSR assistance.[20] Significant differences in norm trajectories between the EU and third countries, suspicion and a lack of local – elite buy-in to EU norms are some of the variables that could (partially) explain norm hybridisation.[21] Norm hybridisation raises doubts about the EU's ability to implement new norms via SSR reforms in different cultural contexts, and within a usual short two to three year programme cycle.[22] Moreover, the recent approach of 'principled-pragmatism', has raised a new critique that the EU is back-peddling on its normative commitments, privileging its own security, neighbourhood and hard power, over democratisation.[23]

Against this background, this paper questions the EU's normative actorness via SSR programmes, and in particular, how key EU norms such as inclusivity, local ownership and gender equality are operationalised via SSR in Mali through the EUCAP Sahel–Mali mission. The paper analyses two stages of the EUCAP Sahel mission- planning and implementation, and two key activities of the mission – training/capacity building and *outreach*.

The EU's case for SSR in Mali

Mali is one of the largest countries in Africa, located in the south of the Sahara. It has a population of 17,994,837 inhabitants, of which 49.97% are women.[24] In addition, a large proportion of persons (66.2%) are under the age of 25 years. Economically, it is one of the poorest countries in the world. Mali takes the 179th place in the Human Development Index (2015) despite being the 'donor darling' in Africa.[25] The complex and ever deepening security crisis experienced by Mali since 2012 is a manifestation of combination of economic, political and other governance deficits. The deteriorating security conditions are alluded to ongoing contestations between various armed groups for power and territorial control and the state's struggles against the increase in non-state armed groups. Various alliances formed between local Jihadist groups and Al-Qaeda, and organisations supported by Arab countries are blamed for Mali's worsening security crisis. At the beginning, the security crisis was largely limited to the remote areas where the state was starkly absent. Today, it is rapidly spreading to the capital and other

[19]S.Panebianco, 'The constraints to EU action as a 'norm entrepreneur' in the Mediterranean, paper presented at the ECPR Joint Sessions of Workshops themed New Roles for the European Union in International Politics (2004).
[20]U.C.Schroeder, F Chappuis and D.Kocak,'Security Sector Reform and the Emergence of Hybrid Security Governance', *International Peacekeeping*, 21, no.2 (2014):217.
[21]U.C.Schroeder and F.Chappuis 'New Perspectives on Security Sector Reform: The Role of Local Agency and Domestic Politics', *International Peacekeeping*, 21 (2): 133,148 (2014):137.
[22]Jayasundara-Smits (2015).
[23]Biscop (2016):92.
[24]World Bank 2016 figures at: https://data.worldbank.org/country/mali.
[25]I.Bergamaschi 'The Fall of a Donor Darling: The Role of Aid in Mali's Crisis', *Journal of Modern African Studies*, 52, no.3 (2014):347–378.

urban areas. Initially, with the help of the French military action (Operation Serval[26]), the Malian state was able to recapture some of the territories lost in the North (Gao, Timbuktu and Kidal) from the armed rebel groups (i.e. Malian Islamic movement– Ançar Dine). Nevertheless, to date, the overall security situation remains critical.[27] These worsening security conditions demand major reforms to the Malian state's security apparatus as well as finding effective governance arrangements to address the underlying complex and multiple causes of the multiple crises hit by Mali.

EUCAP Sahel–Mali mission: scope and functions

The EU has long been a key development donor to Mali.[28] However, under the heightened security crisis (since 2012), the EU began to increase assistance via the Comprehensive Regional Approach (2013) and Action Plan (2015) for the Sahel region by interlinking security, development and governance.[29]

In 2015, the EU established EUCAP Sahel–Mali as a civilian support mission, in addition to the European Union Training Mission (EUTM) that had been operational since February 2013. The main mandate of the EUCAP Sahel mission was to provide strategic advice and training to the three Malian internal security forces, i.e. the police, the Gendarmerie and the National Guard and to the relevant ministries,[30] with the perspective of 'modernising' the Malian security sector. The EUCAP advisors are assigned to help their Malian counterparts to improve their national strategy for human resources, to modernise management practices and control of their services, and with the successfully recruitment of new staff within the Police, the Gendarmerie and the National Guard. As one could note, these activities are concerns with technical capacity building in the security sector. Mission's other related activities such as developing a human resources database, an employment policy and staff management database, a baseline for staffing, a skills-based staff recruitment policy, operational management methods to help restore hierarchical links, audit and inspection units within the general forces inspectorate, are targeting nothing other than bureaucratic uniformity and the functional imperative. Worryingly, the second phase of the mission (extended till 2019) shows increased focus on functional imperative and sliding away from the normative commitments. The newly introduced activities of strengthening the internal security forces' capacity to fight against terrorism and organised crime and supporting Mali in managing migration flows and border management[31] provide

[26]This mission was undertaken by France in January 2013 following the United Nations Security Council Resolution 2085 in December 2012 and an official request from the Malian interim government for French assistance (United Nations Security Council, 'Security Council Press Statement on Mali' (2013).

[27]UN Security Council Press Statement 6 October 2017, https://www.un.org/press/en/2017/sc13019.doc.htm.

[28]J.Carlsson, G.Somolekae and N. Van de Walle. Foreign Aid in Africa: Learning from Country Experiences, Nordiska Africinstutet, Uppsala (1997):145.

[29]Rapid launch of three SSR specific missions – EUTM, EUCAP Niger Sahel and EUCAP Sahel mission is seen as part of the EU's instrumental response to the Malian security crisis, which is intertwined with the EU's own security dilemma and the need for combatting combined effects of the humanitarian catastrophe, security challenges and the risk of large numbers of refugees coming to the EU. R.Gowan, 'Bordering On Crisis: Europe, Africa, and A New Approach to Crisis Management', Brief Policy, European Council on Foreign Relations (2017).

[30]EEAS (June 2016).

[31]EU Official website of the mission https://eucap-sahel-mali.eu/.

evidence to this effect. These two specific activities are built on the logic of 'securitisation' thus enabling to by-pass the established norms and the rules.[32] However, given the EU's overall approach to SSR, still one could assume all these activities to be undertaken, respecting the EU's normative principles underlying SSR. Yet, given the EU's recent eagerness to pursue a principled-pragmatic approach to crisis intervention as announced in its Global Strategy on Foreign and Security Policy (2016), pragmatism taking a precedence over the 'principled' is forewarned too.[33]

As illustrated above, the overall mission is increasingly lacking in the balance between the functional and the normative imperative. This seems to be the case especially in the background of worsening security conditions in the Sahel region emanating from terrorism and increased irregular migration to Europe (least, according to the EU's interpretation). Given the complexity, enormity and pervasiveness of these challenges which the EU mission continued to grapple with, to an extent, one could understand the EU's inclination towards pragmatism. However, the long-term effects of EU's current approach in realising its normative commitments are a valid concern. Therefore, it is pertinent to find out what the EU does/ could do to operationalise SSR specific norms – inclusivity and local ownership in mission planning, implementation and evaluation and through its' everyday activities. In the following section, we analyse to what extent the mission planning was undertaken respecting these two norms, the challenges faced in doing so and the long and short term effects of (non) realisation.

Mission planning: inclusions–exclusions and implications for norm (non) realisation

The planning process of the EUCAP mission was undertaken respecting the principle of inclusivity.[34] The overall goals and the content of the mission was decided in-line with the National Strategies (Plan pour la reliance durable du Mali-PRED2013-2014) presented by the Malian state authorities.[35] The EU's planning process was aimed at maximising the local engagement and ownership of the reform process, as well as eventually holding the Malian counterparts responsible for the mission's outcomes. However, there are a number of issues identified in relation to the degree of ownership and inclusivity of the EU's approach during mission planning. The exclusion of some local actors meant the planning process fell short on its aim of inclusivity. Although the planning documents mention involving civil society in planning, its role is limited to a supporting and a contributory actor to the mission, and it was excluded in terms of subjectivities –

[32]B.Buzan, O.Waever and J.De Wilde.Security, *A New Framework for Analysis* (London: Lynne Rienner Publishers Inc. (1998):23.

[33]Use of EU's new Partnership Framework with Third Countries (EC 2016) is an alarming development where pragmatism is looming larger over the normative in EU policy and practice. This framework is currently used to strike 1–1 deals with a number of rough regimes such as Ethiopia, Turkey, Sudan and Libya to address the EU migration crisis. Although EU has been able significantly reduce the number of migrants arriving at their borders, the deal has come under heavy criticism for sacrificing the international norms and principles in achieving these results.

[34]DCAF and FBF, Country Case Studies to Inform the EU-wide Strategic Framework for Supporting SSR: Findings from Mali, DRC AND Ukraine, Final Report. Geneva, (March 2016):21.

[35]M.Djiré, D.Sow, K.Gakou and B.Camara, Assessing the EU's conflict prevention and peacebuilding interventions in Mali. Bamako: Université des Sciences Juridiques et Politiques de Bamako (2016):7.

ideas, norms and visions. Furthermore, the non-involvement of actors from the Northern part of the country during the consultation process[36] is notable. Such exclusions can be counterproductive inasmuch as they create the risk of competing and overlapping types of security governance arrangements at local level, which are based on different religious and family structures.[37] Although largely informal, these security arrangements are found to be effective. The role they play in providing security in the remote areas-where the state is absent appear vital.[38] Exclusion of these actors and the favouring of a top–down model based on EU standards marginalise and reject the local episteme of security and make local communities passive recipients or subordinates of the external model. Furthermore, the process followed by the EU-represented marginalisation of the northern population, already a source of grievance among people in this part of the country. One fear is that this could contribute to escalate the current security crisis as the marginalised northern actors resort to violence to express and draw attention to their grievances. It also increases the risk that following a traditional 'train and equip' approach could stimulate the competition for power and hegemony between different elite groups as they attempt to capture the new security institutions.

The EU also compromised its own norms by co-opting, by pushing its own security agenda above local demands and needs. Furthermore, it was claimed that the EU pressured local elites to comply with its own priorities.[39] The new mission goals of strengthening of the internal security forces' capacity in the fight against terrorism and organised crime, support for managing migration flows and border management[40] not only reflected a privileging of the EU's security interests, which is at odds with the norm of local ownership. The EU was also criticised for concluding 'deals' with the local elites,[41] which resulted in strengthening the repressive powers of the local elites and exacerbating governance deficits. Thus, new security arrangements that emerge through such a bargaining process run the risk of establishing 'ceremonial' security institutions which lack any value proposition imbued in them.[42]

Mission execution: training and capacity building

The next section looks at how inclusivity was encouraged and/or prevented by the mission as part of its training and capacity building activities.

[36]Nevertheless the Algeria brokered a peace deal 'Agreement for Peace and Reconciliation in Mali, resulting from the Algiers Process" (also known as the 'Bamako Agreement') signed in 2015 included an alliance of Tuareg-led rebels and the Malian State representatives. The implementation of the peace process is far behind schedule and its achievements so far are very little A.Boutellis and Marie-Joëlle Zahar, ' Process in Search of Peace: Lessons from the Inter-Malian Agreement,' New York: International Peace Institute (2017):2.

[37]J. Aulin and C.Divin, 'Towards Local Ownership of International Interventions in Mali', Policy Note, Issue 1, Global Partnership for the Prevention of Armed Conflict, The Hague (2017).

[38]Aulin and Divin (2017).

[39]ibid.

[40]EC, PRESS RELEASE 8/17 11/01/2017 EUCAP Sahel Mali: mission extended for two years, €29.7 million budget adopted.

[41]M.Barnett and C.Zürcher, 'The Peacebuilders Contract: How External State-building Reinforces Weak Statehood', in The Dilemmas of Statebuilding: Confronting the Contradictions of Post-war Peace Operations, eds. R. Paris and T. Sisk (2009): 13–52.

[42]Ibid:39.

Training and capacity development are the main objectives of the EUCAP Sahel mission. In order to reach these goals, the mission uses a training and capacity building curriculum. As the mission website[43] states, the EUCAP Sahel training and capacity building activities are developed 'jointly with the United Nations Multidimensional Integrated Stabilisation Mission in Mali (MINUSMA) and the EUTM Mali military training mission in order to optimise support for the Malian state'. This approach raises many issues. First, it implies limitations in a training curriculum intended for civilian purposes, conducted by a military mission. Second, such an approach prioritises the superiority of military's knowledge and values over that of the civilian. On one hand, this approach may help to socialise the Malian security forces in terms of the international system, doctrines and the international norms. At the same time, it could distance them from local communities, their realities and assessments of security threats at everyday level. The latter is already reflected in the content of the training provided. The EUCAP training curriculum covers a large number of technical subjects, such as management and command, professional ethics, intelligence techniques, professional intervention, criminal policing, counter-terrorism and public order.[44] The training curriculum gives little attention to norm-related topics. At present, they are limited to training on the topics 'Human Rights and Gender.'[45]

The EUCAP training programmes target the staff at senior and the intermediate levels. Each selected staff member receives 100 h of individual training on all topics, over a period of 4 weeks. So far, about 1600 security personals have undergone the programme. The training programme also has a training of trainers (TOT) component. The goal of TOT is to promote local ownership of the training programme. With the support of the EU training advisers, the participants are selected by the commanders of the Malian three internal civilian forces. Due to the culture of 'following orders' in the armed forces, undergoing the EUCAP training programme appears obligatory than voluntary. The obligatory character of the training thus raises issues of varying degrees of interest and commitment to different subject matters by the participants. Without giving a chance to voluntarily enlist, there is no way of knowing participants' underlying motivations for taking part in the training programme. It may well be the case that the seriously impoverished Malian soldiers, finding the components of weapons and technical training more attractive over the normative part. Previous incidents of mass dissertation by several US-trained battalions (including the 2012 coup leader Captain Amadou Sanogo) upon completing a US-led anti-terror training programme, the trained soldiers eventually joining the National Movement for the Liberation of Azawad (MNLA) and committing mass atrocities against the Tuaregs and Arabs illustrate negative examples of the related motivational dimension.[46] Recalling this particular incident, Prof. Goita shared, 'As far as I'm aware, more than 80 Malian soldiers deserted after the training course, taking their weapons and baggage with them'.[47]

---

[43]EUCAP official website https://eucap-sahel-mali.eu/.

[44]EUCAP official website https://eucap-sahel-mali.eu/.

[45]In terms of offering training on gender and Human rights, Mali paints a crowded scenario, where many international, regional and civil society organisations are conducting such training courses for the Malian security forces, and the civil society organisations (i.e. MINUSMA, UN Women and UNFPA, Beyond Peace) .

[46]P.Hatcher, 'French general urges EU to equip "impoverished" Mali army', Reuters (20February 2013).

[47]K.Gänsler, EU military training in Mali (2013), at: http://p.dw.com/p/17Qrr .

The criteria applied for selecting participants also point to a compromise of the normative principles of local ownership and inclusivity. As the mission documents reveal, themed-level and higher officials are the main target groups of the trainings. From the point of view of the EU and of the Malian authorities, there are justifiable reasons for this choice. For instance, targeting higher level officials is important for buy-in to the programme, to counter internal resistance and create conditions for local ownership and responsibility.[48] Excluding higher officials creates mal-functioning security sector institutions, and instances of 'loose coupling' between what is formal and what is the actual day-to-day practice.[49] Having a more inclusive enrolment strategy that targets the security actors at the bottom of the hierarchy is important, while excluding front line cadres who interact with local communities is a missed opportunity to learn from their everyday experiences in understanding and addressing local security needs. In this way, the mission lost an opportunity to integrate their experience and (tacit) inputs for designing the training programme and making it 'relevant' in addressing complex real life security challenges.[50] As Gordon argued, including the security actors from the bottom of the hierarchy is useful for building genuine local ownership, addressing local needs and increasing trust, confidence and legitimacy of security institutions.[51]

As mentioned before, there was an imbalance between the technical and normative parts of the EUCAP training curriculum. Ninety-five per cent of the overall curriculum consists of technical subjects. Only two topics (Human Rights and Gender) cover normative aspects. Therefore, for the Malian soldiers who take part in the training programme, the marginal attention given to the norm-related subjects in the curriculum may mean superiority of technical over the normative. It could also mean EU losing out of an important opportunity in achieving its combined functional-normative values of preparing well-trained soldiers who also fight respecting human rights, avoiding unlawful practices, not engaging in torture and rape. Also, the content of the two norm-related topics deals with the legal backgrounds of these subjects (International Humanitarian Law and United Nations Frameworks for Gender Equality).[52] In addition, even the trainers who delivered the normative parts of the curriculum expressed their deep dissatisfaction with the overbearing nature of the combat and intelligence-related subjects in the curriculum. They are also not satisfied with the format of the training delivery that compartmentalises the normative and the technical subjects.[53] The strict separation between the technical and normative subjects

[48]Jayasundara-Smits and L.Schirch (2015):18.

[49]Schroeder and Kocak:217.

[50]Author's previous personal experiences in conducting Human Rights training programmes (2005–2007) for Sri Lanka's military and the police by separating the higher officers from the soldiers indicates several gaps. On one hand, separate training was an effective strategy to foster an environment for full participation of the each group of participants without prejudice and by overcoming the 'hierarchy' in these establishments. On the other hand, it was also a lost opportunity in fostering collaborative partnerships between different rungs and in developing empathy to each other's roles and tasks.

[51]Schroeder and Chappuis, 'New Perspectives on Security Sector Reform:', 1.

[52]This shows similarity with the reflections from the ISSAT, the main training provider for the EUTAM training mission on International Humanitarian Law and Human Rights. As the project reflection paper notes, the design and the delivery of the military training curriculum taking priority over the Human rights trainings and the ratio of military versus Human rights trainers was 185:1 (http://issat.dcaf.ch/Learn/SSR-in-Practice/Countries-Regions/Mali?view=resources).

[53]ibid.

is also problematic as it misses the simultaneous interactive dynamics between the norms and the functions. Against the general passive learning culture in Mali, achieving the normative goals with this particular format is challenging. As one EU trainer (technical) who conducted a practical training session on police forensic investigation exercise commented, despite their enthusiasm to learn, the Malian participants are spectators than active participants.[54]

With regard to inclusivity, as a whole, the EUCAP training and its related technical and normative components were mainly delivered by the EU member states and their northern civil society counterparts. For instance, Human Rights training was mostly delivered by a French civil society organisation 'Beyond Peace'.[55] According to the recent documents, the HR training is also delivered in partnership with EUTM, MINUSMA and international human rights organisations: ICRC and UN Women.[56] The choice of northern civil society organisations in delivering the normative parts of the curriculum is noteworthy here. At the outset, the heavy involvement of the northern CSOs signals out a cultural connotation. As Lederach reminds us, training is one key element of capacity building and it is about selling 'social' knowledge.[57] 'Selling social knowledge' requires concientisation– awareness of self in context and promoting both personal and social transformation in the participants.[58] Therefore, when crossing cultural boundaries in training, it is crucial to deploy trainers from a mixture of cultural backgrounds.[59] Solely assigning the northern organisations to deliver, especially the normative content of the training (or in other words 'selling cultural knowledge') not only excludes local actors, it also means exclusion of different knowledge traditions and epistemes. By side-lining the local actors– hence local norms and cultures and practices – the mission's training activities seemed to have missed out on an important opportunity for dialogue and (re) negotiation or co-invention of new norms that are acceptable, meaningful and implementable in the local context.

Outreach activities: the matter of gender

In this section, we analyse outreach as one of the key activities undertaken by the EUCAP Sahel–Mali mission. Outreach activities provide an important public space for the EU to demonstrate its commitment and consistent application of its own norms in everyday activities of the mission, thus demonstrating its normative actorness. Outreach activities of the mission are used here to illustrate how and to what extend the EU's normative actorness is achieved/compromised through practice of gender equality – a norm that is being repeatedly affirmed in EU policy documents.[60] Gender equality is integral to local ownership and inclusivity, because it cuts across all the norms underpinning SSR (human rights, good

[54]European Gendarmerie Force, 'A look inside EUCAP Sahel Mali' at: http://www.eurogendfor.org.
[55]ISSAT .
[56]DCAF and FBF (2016):24.
[57]J.P.Lederach, Preparing for Peace: Conflict Transformation Across Cultures, Syracuse University press. (1996):6.
[58]Lederach (1996):19.
[59]Lederach (1996):23.
[60]M.Villellas, Pamela Urrutia, Ana Villellas, Vicenç Fisas, Gender in EU Conflict Prevention and Peacebuilding Policy and Practice, Escola de Cultura de Pau,Barcelona (2016):15. This is also endorsed by the landmark UN Security Council Resolution 2151 on SSR.

governance, and democracy) and sits in every intersection of all social relationships, relations of power.[61] Gender equality is an important normative criterion of measuring the success of SSR programmes. It is not because men and women experience security differently, but also because the security institutions must be representative and equally responsive to the needs of both men and women and owned by both men and women.[62]

However, gender equality is not an easily transferable norm across cultures.[63] In order to realise gender equality, the EUCAP mission needed to think 'outside the box'. Outreach provides an opportunity for tapping into neglected or seemingly invisible 'everyday spaces' to communicate/practice norms regularly. It can be an important and subtle means for debating, assessing, reflecting and renegotiating norms in the local context.

Using the mission's publicly available outreach documents[64] (which focuses on training and capacity building) and by applying the WOS perspective with a focus on the inclusions and exclusions, presences and absences dimensions,[65] this section throws light on how gender equality is being practiced by the mission. A cursory look at the mission's outreach materials suggests however that it lacks sensitivity towards gender equality as a key normative principle. Instead, these documents indicate a reinforcement of gender inequality within the mission, in the capacity building programme and in Malian society. Over representation of men, compared to women in mission's public documents is one of the key issues identified. For instance, at least 90% of the images used in the mission's periodical newsletter – 'La Gazelle'[66] (*Journal d'information de la Mission EUCAP Sahel-Mali*), the foreign male mission staff and their local male counterparts are made hyper visible. These images feed into the existing social stereotypes of 'dominant men'. Furthermore, their presences in the outreach materials are established using images taken mostly during weapons training sessions. Yet again, these images reinforce another social stereotype of 'violent men'. These images do not remain as 'just images', but are being continually mediated by the local cultural and political contexts and by existing relations of power in the Malian society, and hence they have serious normative implications on the Malian society. Furthermore, the absence of women in the outreach materials also reproduces the established stereotypes of women as innocent, vulnerable, marginalised, passive and subjects (victims) of man's violence. By so doing, these materials contribute in making the agency of Malian women invisible. Malian women's presence in the outreach material is more prominent on topics related to civil society, human rights and gender-related activities. These

---

[61]Gordon, Welch & Roos, 'Security Sector Reform and the Paradoxical Tension', 4.

[62]L.Schirch (with Mancini-Griffoli, Deborah), Local Ownership in Security: Case Studies of Peacebuilding Approaches. The Hague: Alliance for Peacebuilding, GPPAC, Kroc Institute (2015):8.

[63]This is also the case with other norms underpinning SSR such as democracy, good governance, human rights.

[64]Mission website contains other documents such as factsheets, guidelines with dealing with victims of violence against women and girls and the handbooks on Criminal Code, on Border Management and on Violence against women and girls.

[65]Visual analysis of the newsletter was conducted using media and visual analysis tools of Framing and Focalisation. See C.B.Schwalbe, 'Remembering our Shared Past: Visually Framing the Iraq War on US News Websites', *Journal of Computer-Mediated Communication*, 12, no.1 (2006):264–289; M. Meijer, 'Countering textual violence: On the critique of representation and the importance of teaching its methods', Women's studies international forum, Elsevier (1993):367–378.

[66]There are four newsletters issues so far, Issue no.1 (14 January 2016), no:2 (May 2016), and no.3 (January 2017) and no.4 (May 2017).

images thus reproduce new societal stereotypes of women (particularly in places Western interventions are taking place), as accomplices of the west's intrusive liberal peace project. Regular presences of white-western women as 'training providers' in these materials also recast what Paris cited as 'mission civilisatrice'.[67] Portraying white-western women in superior positions recast black-local men (and women) as powerless, uneducated, immature and passive subjects. These numerous visibilities and invisibilities enacted through the images in the mission's outreach materials recast the societal race–gender power relations as well.[68] Taken together, these numerous presences and absences and particular instances of presences and absences compromise the principles of inclusiveness, local ownership and gender norms.

Conclusion

Applying the WOS approach, this paper has shown how two key SSR norms of local ownership and inclusivity (inclusive of gender equality) presented operational challenges for the EUCAP Sahel–Mali mission. These challenges were identified at two levels: first at the level of overall Malian context (broad) and second at the mission's operational level (specific). Realising and internalising norms was found to be more difficult against the background of a worsening security crisis in Mali and in the Sahel region which contributed to distracting the EU and their local partners from the normative goals of SSR. This situation is further encouraged by the EU's 'principled-pragmatic' approach to crisis intervention, reflected in the activities of the mission's second mandate.

From the perspective of WOS, viewing the mission through the prism of the vertical (inclusiveness of actors) and the horizontal axes (practices) this paper captured the overtly functional- instrumental nature of the EUCAP Sahel–Mali mission. The mission's main objective – training a third of the staff of the internal security forces in over four weeks, underlines the mission's preference for applying a short term, top–down functional approach rather than a longer term normative – governance–development approach. This was further demonstrated in the activities of the second phase of the mission that largely focus on counter-terrorism and border management. These activities show how the mission prioritises EU security interests over local security considerations, suggesting both a lack of inclusivity and local ownership and exclusion and marginalisation of local actors during the planning processes (and even co-optation and manipulation of some of the key actors) who have important stakes in the Malian security scenario.

By delving into the mission's training activities and modalities of their delivery, this paper traced various instances of inclusions, exclusions and marginalisations of actors and the norms. The imbalance (between normative and functional subjects) in the training curriculum and the mission's inability to itself demonstrate its own norms of inclusivity and gender equality when it came to building training teams and the selection of participants was significant. Although improved gender sensitivity is

[67]R.Paris, 'International Peacebuilding and the "Mission Civilisatrice"',. *Review of International Studies*, 28, no.4 (2002):638.

[68]This finding also echoes Spivak's observations on how the 'white' Western wo/man gender expert takes the role of saving 'brown/local' wo/men victims (*Op Cit.*, in Kunz (2014):610.

suggested by normative considerations, including more women in missions and utilising their agency has also been seen to increase the functional effectiveness in other cases of SSR missions. These examples show how women can help gain trust and acceptance more easily from the local communities and act as effective carrier of normative messages.[69]

The analysis of the mission's public outreach documents suggests how the mission could be an effective vehicle for norm diffusion by focusing on how information is shared rather than the kind of information provided. A WOS approach suggests that the mission could have pursued a more inclusive approach by considering segments such as the Northern populations, and women in the training and outreach activities. In addition, by reviewing their training and outreach activities against local practices and by aligning more closely with best practices on gender at international level, and by integrating national plans and priorities on issues such as inclusivity, use of the horizontal WOS axis could have improved the mission's normative focus.

Overall, these findings suggest the need to acknowledge and engage more deeply with the normative implications and the underlying political dimension and context of the mission. A deeper level of political engagement is crucial if the mission is to make an impact on Malian society and its social–political institutions. By delving deeper into the mission specific activities (planning and implementation-training and outreach) this paper was also able to identify a number of issues in operationalising and realising the EU's own norms, which in turn challenge the EU's overall credibility as a normative actor. However the mission specific challenges are easier to address by adjusting everyday activities, and here, a WOS perspective, would highlight opportunities to counter the incidence of exclusions, invisibilities and marginalisation in terms of actors and norms. A WOS approach could strengthen the rhetorical commitments and restore the EU's diminishing reputation as a normative actor.

Abbreviations

CSDP	– Common Security and Defence Policy
CSO	– Civil Society Organisation
EU	– European Union
EUCAP	– Sahel Mali – European Capability Building Mission Sahel Mali
EUTM	– European Union Training Mission
ICRC	– The International Committee of the Red Cross
MINUSMA	– United Nations Multidimensional Integrated Stabilisation Mission in Mali
MNLA	– National Movement for the Liberation of Azwad
OECD	– Organisation for Economic Co-operation and Development
SSR	– Security Sector Reform
TOT	– Training of Trainers
WOS	– Whole of Society

[69]J.O'Neill and J. Vary, 'Allies and Assets: Strengthening DDR and SSR through Women's Inclusion' in Monopoly of Force: The Nexus of DDR and SSR, edds. Melanne A. Civic and Michael Miklaucic (The National DEFENCE University, Washington D.C 2011):94; S.Jayasundara-Smits, Civil-Military Synergy at Operational Level in EU External Action, WOSCAP-EU, Global Partnership for the Prevention of Armed Conflict (GPPAC), The Hague (2016):22.

Acknowledgment

Author would like to thank the anonymous peer-reviewers for their helpful comments, Dr. Vesna Bojičić-Dželilović and Dr.Mary Martin at LSE for their advise and critical comments during various stages of writing of this article.

Disclosure statement

No potential conflict of interest was reported by the author.

Funding

This work was supported by the European Union's Horizon 2020 Research and Innovation Programme [grant number 653866.

ORCID

Shyamika Jayasundara-Smits http://orcid.org/0000-0002-1022-269X

Coordinating international interventions in complex settings. An analysis of the EU peace and state-building efforts in post-independence Kosovo

Chris van der Borgh, Puck le Roy and Floor Zweerink

ABSTRACT

This paper assesses coordination as a salient capability of international interventions in complex settings characterised by weak states, the dominance of political elites whose interest in reforms is questionable and multiple local and international stakeholders. It focuses on the challenge of integrating a range of national and international actors and multiple policy domains, assessing this operational capability in terms of a Whole-of-Society approach. Using the example of the EU's intervention in Kosovo through the mechanisms of the EULEX mission, and the EU-facilitated Dialogue between Serbia and Kosovo, the paper argues that the EU's impact in Kosovo was weakened by its limited ability to include and engage a broad range of local stakeholders. While a Whole-of-Society approach could address this weakness, the paper also argues that a better understanding of the context-specific opportunities and limitations placed on international organisations like the EU is needed.

Introduction

Over the past 20 years, the EU has transformed from an actor with limited leverage to a major player in Kosovo. Arguably, there is no other country where the EU plays a more central role in the processes of state building and stabilisation than in Kosovo. This paper discusses the EU's capabilities to coordinate with national and international stakeholders. Coordination is an important objective of most international actors, such as the UN, involved in state- and peacebuilding operations. It is, however, also widely acknowledged that coordination is often problematic. Roland Paris has noted that the call for improved coordination 'offers soothing simplicity in the face of disturbing complexity', since it often hides the 'disagreements and uncertainties about the means and ends of the entire enterprise'.[1] Therefore, a realistic assessment of coordination and the scope of improvement should not only take into account

[1]Paris, 'Understanding the "coordination problem" in postwar state-building', in Roland Paris and Timothy Sisk, *The dilemmas of statebuilding. Confronting the contradictions of postwar peace operations* (Abingdon, New York: Routledge, 2009), p. 53.

complexity, but depart from it. Complexity refers both to the context of intervention[2] and to the peace operations themselves.[3]

This paper analyses international intervention in war-torn societies as essentially contested processes in which reaching consensus about ends and means appears to be extremely difficult and compromise is often flimsy at best. This has implications for the ideal of a Whole-of-Society (WoS) approach, which claims that better coordination will lead to better outcomes of interventions. For the capability to coordinate to be viable, there is a need for a deeper awareness of the contradictory interests and views about post-war societies and the tensions and contradictions between different reform processes. Therefore, the capability to coordinate should not be seen as a 'technique', but rather as a 'politics' of international actors.

The structure of this paper is as follows. It first reviews the academic discussion on coordination between national and international actors in general and the discussion about EU capabilities to coordinate in particular. It moves on with a short discussion of the years before Kosovo's independence, when the UN was the leading external actor, which already faced many of the problems that the EU would also be confronted with at a later stage. The next section focuses on the post-independence period when the EU started to play a prominent role in the process of state- and peacebuilding. The focus is on two of the most important EU interventions in Kosovo: the EULEX mission and the EU-facilitated Dialogue between Serbia and Kosovo. The paper closes with a reflection on the WoS approach.

Forging and contesting capabilities

The WoS approach seeks to encompass the complex dynamics of the conflict and post-conflict environment through problematising not only the multi-actor environment but also the integration of different policies and peacebuilding actions across a broad spectrum of security needs.[4] It refers to the EU's capabilities to synchronise their agendas with other international actors ('international coordination') and with local stakeholders, including warring parties, governments and civil society (inclusivity). While the need for international coordination has been stressed by international actors over the past decades, inclusivity is an emerging norm within international policy processes.[5] This paper deals with the capability to coordinate with international- and national-level actors.

A capability is about the ability and capacity to achieve objectives in relation to the overall mission of an international organisation or any other actor that is able to make policy. It has to be understood in relation to expectations and ambitions with regard to stated (policy) goals. The higher the expectations and ambitions regarding the goals, the

[2] J. Goodhand and D. Hulme, 'From Wars to Complex Political Emergencies: Understanding Conflict and Peace-Building in the New World Disorder', *Third World Quarterly*, 20, no. 1 (1999), 15–16.

[3] C. Clement and A. C. Smith, eds., *Managing Complexity: Political and Managerial Challenges in United Nations Peace Operations* (New York: International Peace Institute, July 2009), https://www.ipinst.org/wp-content/uploads/publications/complexity_1.pdf; C.T. Hunt, *UN Peace Operations and International Policing. Negotiating Complexity, Assessing Impact and Learning To Learn* (Abingdon, New York: Routledge, 2015).

[4] M. Martin, V. Bojicic-Dzelilovic, C. van der Borgh and G. Frerks, Theoretical and Methodological Framework (London: London School of Economics and Political Science and Utrecht: Utrecht University, 2016), 14.

[5] T. Donais and E. McCandless, 'International peace building and the emerging inclusivity norm, *Third World Quarterly* 38, no. 2 (2017): 291–310.

greater the capabilities needed to realise these.[6] With the growing number of peace operations and their more complex mandates after the cold war, the question of coordination has gained importance and is considered a capability in its own right.[7] This is also the case for the EU, whose expectations regarding inclusivity and comprehensiveness are quite high and form a leitmotif in its policies. The Comprehensive Approach to security is the way the EU seeks to operationalise these ideas.[8] It is, however, widely recognised that implementation raises a range of challenges 'at the politico-strategic level, at the level of operational and policy planning and in day-to-day implementation'.[9]

In their framework to analyse capabilities, Whitman and Wolff emphasise that capabilities should be understood in their respective contexts (the context–capability nexus).[10] The authors make a distinction between four types of context: local, national, regional and global and the need to deal with different actor constellations and challenges at each of these levels.[11] Furthermore, three types of capabilities are identified that the EU needs in order to be effective: the capability to act, to fund and to coordinate and cooperate.[12] With regard to coordination and cooperation, the authors focus on the capability to coordinate between international actors, while emphasising the need to take into account local actors and to 'determine the relevant players and analyse in detail their interests and capabilities and on the basis of this begin to build as broad a coalition as possible in support of an outcome-oriented process'.[13] This implies that, in order to be effective, coordination and cooperation with other actors – aligning different interests and agendas – are key to international intervention. In other words, most actions of international agents require the inputs, consent or agreement of a range of other actors – both local and international. The possibilities and limitations to do so depend on the relevant contexts.

In the academic literature, calls for inclusiveness and comprehensiveness of international peace- and state-building policies have been critically examined.[14] Discussing the efforts of international actors to coordinate their policies, Paris warns against seeing coordination as a 'technique' to overcome the often disappointing outcomes of peace and state-building interventions.[15] The concept suggests a pre-existing consensus and insufficiently takes into account strategic disagreements over state-building, the political roles played by international interveners and the complexities of local societies and power dynamics (ibid). The EU is not unaware of this and proclaims to use its 'soft

[6]Martin, Theoretical and Methodological Framework.
[7]R. Whitman and S. Wolff, eds., *The European Union as a Global Conflict Manager* (Abingdon, New York: Routledge, 2012): 11.
[8]C. Gebhard and P. Norheim-Martinsen, 'Making Sense of EU Comprehensive Security towards Conceptual and Analytical Clarity', *European Security*, 20, no. 2 (2011): 221.
[9]Ibid.,221.
[10]Whitman and Wolff, *The European Union*, 213.
[11]Ibid, 14–17.
[12]Ibid, 11.
[13]Ibid, 218.
[14]C. Castillejo, Dilemmas and experiences of international support for inclusive peacebuilding, Report (Oslo: Noref, 2017). file:///C:/Users/Chris/Downloads/Castillejo_Dilemmas%20and%20experiences%20of%20international%20support%20for%20inclusive%20peacebuilding_Oct2017_final.pdf; V. Dudouet and S. Lundström, Post-war Political Settlements. From Participatory Transition Process to Inclusive State-building and Governance, Research Report (Berlin: Berghof Foundation, 2016).
[15]Paris, 'Understanding', 58–60.

power' through non-coercive measures aimed at gaining the consent of other stakeholders in policy implementation.[16] However, interventions are fundamentally contested processes in which the interests of international, national and subnational actors often widely differ.[17] Hence, the different actors involved in the interventions are not necessarily 'coordinating', but rather interacting strategically with each other. According to Barnett and Zürcher, the most likely outcome is not consent of local actors, but a 'compromise' between the different stakeholders that only superficially reflects the agendas of international actors.[18]

These sobering accounts of the possibilities of coordination, comprehensiveness and inclusion (in Kosovo and beyond) raise the question to what outcomes coordination and negotiations between different national and international elites lead. We do not assume that the interests of different stakeholders are necessarily incompatible, or fixed, but rather follow Colebatch's view of policy as structured interaction.[19] In this view, policy should not simply be seen as the pursuit of 'shared goals', but also as the more difficult task of negotiating and constructing a basis for collective action among participants with quite diverse views on the nature of the task.[20] The analysis of intervention requires a reconstruction of the interactions between the relevant players in a given 'policy area' or 'policy arena'. These can be players that are directly involved, but also stakeholders that would like to be included.[21] Zooming in on these relations provides more detailed insight in the ways in which capabilities develop, adapt, grow or erode in complex and largely unpredictable processes.

In the sections below, we analyse the strategic manoeuvring of the EU in Kosovo, focusing on two of its most important interventions there: the EU mission and the EU-facilitated Dialogue. These sections are based on a more elaborate analysis, which traced these interventions, focusing on the interactions between actors, and the resulting adaptation in (international) policies.[22] In our analysis, we made a distinction between policy design, policy implementation and policy change and adaptation.[23] For each stage, the relevant actions of the EU were identified, the relevant interactions with other stakeholders, and the outcomes of policy measures as assessed by different stakeholders.[24] In that process, local and international interests and agendas are not separate and fixed but influence each other, and

[16]K. Nielsen, 'EU Soft Power and the Capability-expectations Gap', *Journal of Contemporary European Research*, 9, no. 5 (2013): 723–39.

[17]M. Barnett and C. Zürcher 'The Peacebuilders Contract: How External State-Building Reinforces Weak Statehood', in Paris and Sisk, *The dilemmas of state-building* (2009), 13–52; A. de Waal, 'Mission Without End? Peacekeeping in the Political Marketplace', in *International Affairs*, 85, no. 1 (2009): 99–113.

[18]Barnett and Zürcher, 'The peacebuilders contract'.

[19]H. Colebatch, *Policy* (Maidenhead: Open University Press/McGraw-Hill Education, 2009), 26.

[20]Ibid.

[21]Ibid., 4.

[22]C. van der Borgh, P. le Roy, and F. Zweerink, EU peacebuilding capabilities in Kosovo after 2008: an analysis of EULEX and the EU-facilitated Belgrade-Pristina Dialogue (Utrecht: Utrecht University, 2017), http://www.woscap.eu/documents/131298403/131299900/Kosovo+report_PU+%285%29.pdf/3f0fb0f7-e81c-4e42-bdee-c43efabfafed. The research is based on a literature review and focuses on the interactions between national and international elites. In addition, in May, June and September 2016, 12 interviews were held in the Netherlands, Brussels and Kosovo with (former) staff of international organisations, local NGO leaders (in Pristina and Mitrovica) and local researchers and journalists.

[23]Martin, Methodological Framework, 35.

[24]Ibid.

they are 'interlocked'.[25] Thus, instead of looking for capability as something dichotomous that external interveners either have or have not, the focus of this paper is on the social processes in which capabilities emerge and erode in (often changing) national and local contexts.

UNMIK's heritage and status issues

With the suspension of NATO's bombing campaign, on 10 June 1999, the UN Security Council passed Resolution 1244, which announced the Council's decision to replace the Federal Republic of Yugoslavia's (FRY) authorities with the deployment of international civil and security presences in Kosovo: the United Nations Interim Administration Mission in Kosovo (UNMIK) and the NATO led Kosovo Force (KFOR). Although Resolution 1244 recognised FRY's sovereignty over Kosovo, UNMIK – an international administration – became the 'de facto' government. While UNMIK was supposed to promote 'meaningful self-governance', the international community postponed the decision on Kosovo's status, which remained a bone of contention between the Serbian minority in Kosovo and the majority Kosovo Albanians.[26]

The immediate post-intervention period in Kosovo (between 1999 and 2008) was characterised by multiple conflicts about Kosovo's status and legitimate governance between local Kosovo-Albanian actors (the Democratic League of Kosovo and the Kosovo Liberation Army), as well as between Serbian and Kosovar groups.[27] In this context, UNMIK faced numerous dilemmas to deal with local actors and to foster local ownership.[28] The international administration of UNMIK was reluctant to take the upper hand and preferred to hide behind a discourse of local ownership.[29] Narten argues that UNMIK chose to work with 'the still powerful, former warring parties that were also engaged in postwar crime activities' and that it 'missed the critical point for a well-balanced identification and strengthening of local partners through a consistent transfer of powers, and by not setting transparent, fair, and realistically achievable benchmarks with clearly defined indicators of achievement for local counterparts'.[30]

Also, there were multiple coordination problems between international actors. With the chaotic organisation of the international community in Bosnia still fresh in everyone's mind, attempts were made to bring more structure into the civil and administrative mission in Kosovo. It was therefore decided to opt for a 'pillar model', with the European Union and the Organisation for Security and Cooperation in Europe (OSCE) reporting to UNMIK. While this was generally regarded as a step forward, it did not prevent 'turf wars' between and within these organisations. King and Mason point to UNMIK's failed attempts to coordinate the activities of the various international

[25]This is a variation on Long and Van der Ploeg's concept of interlocking projects. See N. Long and van der Ploeg, 'Heterogeneity, actor and structure: Towards a reconstitution of the concept of structure', in Booth, D. *Rethinking Social Development: Theory, Research and Practice*, London: Longman, 1994), 62–89.

[26]C. van der Borgh, 'Resisting International State Building in Kosovo', *Problems of Post-Communism, 59*, no. 2 (2012): 31–42.

[27]Ibid.

[28]S. Chesterman *You, The People: The United Nations, Transitional Administration, and State-Building* (Oxford, Oxford University Press, 2004); J. Narten, 'Dilemmas of promoting "local ownership": the case of postwar Kosovo, in Paris and Sisk, *The Dilemmas of Statebuilding*, 252–83.

[29]Chesterman, *You, the People*.

[30]Narten, 'Dilemmas of promoting', 271, 276.

organisations, and the fact that UNMIK was serving too many masters, thereby causing a lack of unity.[31] Indeed, the early years of international intervention in Kosovo showed that consensus about Kosovo's political future and the transitional administration were lacking, which deeply hampered UNMIK's efforts to coordinate. Faced with this problematic political reality, UNMIK delayed transferring power to local institutions and avoided to engage in a discussion on Kosovo's status between 1999 and 2002.[32] This made UNMIK widely unpopular among the Kosovo Albanians, who scornfully referred to the UN mission as 'anmik', which means 'enemy' in Kosovo Albanian.[33]

The absence of a clear road map about the future status of Kosovo 'posed a virtually insurmountable obstacle in the efforts of the international administration to bring lasting peace and stability'.[34] By the year of 2004, events on the ground, including the anti-Serbian riots in March, forced the international community to put the issue of Kosovo's status back on its agenda. In February 2007, Ahtisaari presented his draft 'Comprehensive Status Proposal' (CSP) to both Belgrade and Pristina.[35] The CSP recommended 'conditional independence supervised by the international community, [...] that reintegration into Serbia was not viable, and continued international administration was not sustainable'.[36] The Serbian side rejected the conclusion of the Ahtisaari report. The Serbs living in Kosovo were also very much opposed to the Ahtisaari plan, as they feared Kosovo's independence would ultimately lead to Albanian domination in Kosovo and would result in their loss of the practical and financial advantages of the Serbian state presence in Kosovo.[37]

The EU and the USA initially hoped the UN Security Council would endorse Ahtisaari's CSP with a new resolution that would supersede Resolution 1244, even though Serbia had rejected the draft. When it became clear that the Ahtisaari plan did not receive enough support within the Security Council due to the expected negative veto of Russia and China,[38] the EU unable to define her position towards Kosovo and aware that inaction could damage her reputation, began to consider bypassing the Security Council. Finally, the USA, together with a group of EU Member States, facilitated Kosovo's unilateral declaration of independence, delivered by Kosovo's political representatives on 17 February 2008.[39] The declaration specifically mentioned the Ahtisaari plan, and Kosovo pledged it would fully implement it.[40] In 2008, the International Civilian Office was created to supervise Kosovo's independence. It was headed by Mr Pieter Feith, who had already been appointed the EU Special Representative (EUSR) in Kosovo.[41]

---

[31]I. King and W. Mason, *Peace at Any Price. How the World Failed Kosovo* (London, Hurst and Company, 2006).

[32]G. Visoka, 'International Governance and Local Resistance in Kosovo: the Thin Line between Ethical, Emancipatory and Exclusionary Politics', *Irish Studies in International Affairs, 22* (2011), 99–125.

[33]W. Koeth, 'State Building Without a State: The EU's Dilemma in Defining its Relations With Kosovo', *European Foreign Affairs Review, 15* (2010): 227–47.

[34]Yannis, A, 'The UN as Government in Kosovo', *Global Governance, 10*, no. 1 (2004): 75; Koeth, 'State Building', 231.

[35]Ahtisaari was assisted by two EU officials from both the Council of the European Union and the European Commission.

[36]Koeth, 'State Building Without a State', 232.

[37]F. Bieber, The Serbia-Kosovo Agreements: An EU Success Story? *Review of Central and East European Law, 40* (2015), 285–319.

[38]Visoka, 'International Governance'.

[39]Koeth, 'State Building Without a State'.

[40]F. T. Bislimi, 'International Statebuilding in Kosovo: The Shifting Trend in the Level of US-EU Involvement', *The Western Balkans Policy Review, 2*, no. 2 (2012): 48–72.

[41]International Civilian Office, *State Building and Exit. The International Civilian Office and Kosovo's Supervised Independence 2008–2012* (Pristina: ICO, December 2012), 57.

After 2008, the status issue was still far from settled and continued to plague efforts to bring stability and peace to the region and to build a new Kosovar state. Serbia was not willing to recognise Kosovo's independence and continued its influence in Kosovo by supporting Serbian 'parallel' governance structures. By September 2016, two of the permanent five members of the Security Council – Russia and China – did not recognise Kosovo (111 countries had recognised Kosovo as an independent state).[42] Moreover, 5 of the 27 members of the EU – Spain, Slovakia, Greece, Romania and Cyprus – had not recognised Kosovo's independence either, leading to serious challenges for the EU in dealing with the state. This continuing international disagreement about Kosovo's status continued to hamper the deployment of the international community.

Thus, over the past two decades, a broad range of international organisations have been involved in the management and resolution of the conflict on and in Kosovo. After Kosovo's declaration of independence, the EU stepped up its presence in Kosovo, inheriting a series of structural problems that were not easy to resolve. Kosovo's status was and remained a point of contention between Kosovo and Serbia, within the EU and at international level. The state-building process of Kosovo was seriously hampered by the lack of consensus about Kosovo's status, as well as the high levels of corruption in the country.

EU interventions in Kosovo after 2008

Over the past 20 years, the influence of the EU in Kosovo 'has been expanding gradually into the political, judicial, economic and security spheres'.[43] In the weeks following 10 June 1999, when UNMIK was deployed in Kosovo, the EU agreed to become a stakeholder in the UN mission through financing 'Pillar IV' or 'the EU Pillar' of UNMIK. Completely financed by the European Commission, the EU Pillar, together with the newly established European Agency for Reconstruction and the EU Monitoring Mission of the Council of the EU, made up the EU presence in Kosovo.[44] It was, however, after Kosovo's declaration of independence on 17 February 2008 that the EU took over the most important tasks of Kosovo's rule of law reform.[45]

In this section, two of the most important interventions of the EU will be discussed into more detail: the EULEX mission and the EU-facilitated Dialogue between Serbia and Kosovo. In both, the challenges to coordinate a range of actors were of great importance but were dealt with in different ways. The number of EU interventions and engagements with Kosovo was, however, broader. Particularly important was the Stabilisation and Association Process, which was developed as a common framework for relations with the Western Balkans up to their accession to the European Union. The Stabilisation and Association Agreements (SAA's) served as an important carrot during the dialogue process between Kosovo and Serbia and the SAA with Kosovo

[42]See Republic of Kosovo Ministry of Foreign Affairs. (2016). *International recognitions of the Republic of Kosovo*. Retrieved from Republic of Kosovo Ministry of Foreign Affairs, http://www.mfa-ks.net/?page=2,224.

[43]Krasniqui, G., 2015, 'The EU's Relations with Kosovo – Achievements, Limits, Challenges', European Futures: http://www.europeanfutures.ed.ac.uk/article-2482.

[44]Koeth, 'State Building Without a State'.

[45]Bislimi, 'International Statebuilding in Kosovo'.

entered into force on 1 April 2016.[46] In addition, Kosovo has been one of the most important recipients of European technical and financial cooperation, which was, *inter alia*, used to fund activities of institution building and socio-economic development.[47]

EULEX – compromises, compromises, compromises

Established in 2008, the objectives of the EULEX include the support of the police and judiciary, border management and tackling of corruption and organised crime.[48] With an annual budget of around 76 million Euros[49] in 2016, it is the most expensive mission ever executed by the European Union.[50] On top of that, its partly executive mandate – in addition to its 'strengthening' mandate – also set this EU mission apart from other civilian missions deployed under the CSDP in the Western Balkans.[51] EULEX faced enormous challenges in terms of its capability to coordinate, and the Mission has been extensively criticised, in academic and policy literatures, in formal evaluations and by political leaders in Kosovo and Serbia (albeit for different reasons).[52]

As to the reasons for EULEX's relatively poor performance, there is little doubt that at all levels (local, national, regional and international), the mission encountered serious challenges that influenced its performance. However, the report of the European Court of Accountants published in 2012 emphasised that these 'specific circumstances' could only partly be held responsible for the disappointing results of the EULEX mission.[53] This is a fair point, since a number of organisational problems were responsible for the relatively poor results. For example, EULEX faced problems to contract capable staff and in terms of its administration and its communication strategy. Furthermore, the fact that a civilian mission was initially led by a military staff member was questioned by several (former) staff members of EULEX.[54] In addition, the objective of EULEX to address the rule of law in almost all its dimensions may well have been too ambitious.

[46]P. van Elsuwege, 'Legal Creativity in EU External Relations. The Stabilisation and Association Agreement between Kosovo and the EU', *European Foreign Affairs Review* 22, no. 3 (2017): 393–410. A key development in the framework for the EU's relationship with the candidate and potential candidate countries of the Western Balkans has been visa liberalisation.

[47]Van der Borgh, 'EU peacebuilding capabilities'.

[48]European Court of Auditors, *European Union Assistance to Kosovo Related to the Rule of Law* (Luxembourg: European Court of Auditors, 2012), 11. See for the mission statement Joint Action 2008/124/CFSP.

[49]EULEX (n.d.) 'Basic Facts', http://www.eulex-kosovo.eu/eul/repository/docs/AE20160531_Fact_Sheet_1.2.pdf (accessed June 2, 2016).

[50]S. Laudes and F. Sánchez Andrada, 'EULEX: A mission in need of reform and with no end in sight', (Real Instituto Elcano Royal Institute, 2015), http://www.realinstitutoelcano.org/wps/portal/web/rielcano_en/contenido?WCM_GLOBAL_CONTEXT=/elcano/elcano_es/zonas_es/europa/ari41-2015-llaudes-sanchezandrada-eulex-mission-need-reform-no-end-in-sight .

[51]M. Spernbauer *EULEX Kosovo – Mandate, structure and implementation: Essential clarifications for an unprecedented EU mission* (Brussels: CLEER, 2010).

[52]See S. Bajrami, 'The Rule of Law in Kosovo: Mission impossible?' (Balkan Insight, 2011), http://www.balkaninsight.com/en/article/the-rule-of-law-in-kosovo-mission-impossible; T. Cierco and L. Reis, 'EULEX's impact on the Rule of Law in Kosovo', *Revista de Ciencia Politicia*, 34, no. 3 (2014): 645–63; European Court of Auditors, *European Union Assistance*; Laudes and Sanchez, 'Eulex: A mission in need of reform'; A. Radin 'Analysis of current events: "towards the rule of law in Kosovo: EULEX should go"', *Nationalities Papers*, 42, no. 2 (2014): 181–94. See for a more positive evaluation R. Zupančič, N. Pejič, B. Grilj, and A. Peen Rodt, 'The European Union Rule of Law Mission in Kosovo: An Effective Conflict Prevention and Peace-Building Mission?', *Journal of Balkan and Near Eastern Studies* (2017) http://www.tandfonline.com/doi/pdf/10.1080/19448953.2017.1407539?needAccess=true.

[53]European Court of Auditors, European Union Assistance.

[54]Author's interview with Pieter Feith, Dutch diplomat and former EU Special Representative and International Civilian Representative in Kosovo, 20 June 2016, The Hague.

But although in the given circumstances EULEX could have done more, the complexities of the interconnected local, national and international contexts should not be underestimated. EULEX needed to deal at all these levels with actors that disagreed about the future of Kosovo and the role that EULEX should play.

At the international level, EULEX faced serious coordination problems. Within the EU, there was no consensus about the status of Kosovo, and the head of the EULEX mission had to manage the diverse interests among the 28 member states (with their representations in the political and security committee). In the words of the former EUSR Pieter Feith: 'a big part of my job consisted of compromising, compromising, compromising'.[55] When the EU started to develop EULEX, it assumed that the mandate under which the UN had worked (UNSCR 1244) would be changed. However, the continuing ambiguity and controversy about the status of Kosovo, both at the international level and within the EU, led to renegotiations about the deployment of EULEX and eventually to a 'handicapped'[56] EULEX mission that declared itself to be 'status neutral'. This negatively influenced the effectiveness of EULEX's intervention. These early years of the EULEX mission show that a low capability to coordinate the international position on Kosovo's status (also within the EU) seriously hampers the international capacity to act.

The EULEX mission also encountered serious obstacles in its interactions with national elites. Barnett and Zürcher claim that the counterparts of governance programmes often do not have a genuine interest in the proposed reforms, proved – at least in part – true for the case of Kosovo. While EULEX both aimed at strengthening the Kosovar judicial sector and to take the necessary measures (among others through its executive mandate) to stop corruption, several reports pointed at their problematic implementation.[57] The Marty Report mentioned corruption as a major problem, claiming that the political power of Kosovar elites that allegedly had connections with organised crime, counted on the 'de facto' support of the EU and the USA.[58] The European Court of Auditors (ECA) report shared that view and quoting OSCE studies about the high risk of Kosovo becoming (or even of actually already being) a 'captured state'.[59] It also noted that 'the Kosovo authorities have given a low priority to anti-corruption activities', and it explicitly questioned the political will of the political elites to implement new reforms.[60] Some of the concerns expressed by ECA in the 2012 report were also mentioned in the 'Jacqué Report'.[61] While this report focuses on the allegations of corruption within EULEX and the treatment of alleged whistle-blowers, part of the report discusses the more general implementation of the mandate by EULEX, concluding that 'in its current state Kosovo's judicial system does not seem

55Ibid.

56L. Greicevci, L. 'EU actorness in international affairs: The case of EULEX mission in Kosovo', in *Perspectives on European Politics and Society*, 12, no. 3 (2011): 283–303.

57Barnet and Zürcher, 'The peacebuilders contract'.

58Tolksdorf, D., 2013, EU and U.S. cooperation in rule of law assistance in Kosovo. *Paper prepared for presentation at the 8th Pan-European Conference on International Relations, 18–22 September 2013*. Warsaw, 17.

59European Court of Auditors, European Union Assistance, 22.

60Ibid., 23–24.

61Jacqué, J.-P, *Review of the Eulex Kosovo Mission's Implementation of the Mandate with a particular focus on the handling of the recent allegations. Report to the attention of High Representative / Vice President of the European Commission Ms Federica Mogherini* (2015).

to be capable of meeting the challenges of corruption and the organized crime associated with it'.[62]

Former EU staff recognised the problem of political elites' involvement in organised crime and corruption. Former EUSR Peter Feith argued that EULEX had insufficiently been able to address this, arguing that EULEX also lacked a clear vision of how to achieve this. In this regard, the political support of key EU member states – like Germany and the UK – as well as the USA, to take tougher measures was lacking, since a tougher stance would have come at the cost of stability in Kosovo.[63] This critique was also voiced by Capussela, who summarises the attitude of the West since 1999 as preferring 'to appease, rather than confront, Kosovo's leadership'.[64] In order to implement its 'reform agenda', EULEX (and the EU in general) chose to cooperate with these same political elites that seemed not sincerely interested in it.

It is also striking that, even though EULEX claimed to aim for a 'locally owned' rule of law mission, consultation of Kosovar civil society initially was rather limited. An evaluation of European Peacebuilding Liaison Office (EPLO) about the first years of EULEX concluded that while there were interactions with civil society representatives, these had not been formalised yet and mostly consisted of providing information.[65] The same report mentions that a number of civil society organisations were very critical about EULEX' executive powers and its 'status neutrality'. For example, the CSO *Lëvizja Vetëvendosje* (Self-Determination; which would later become a political party) opposed the presence of EULEX (and of UNMIK). More generally, the report pointed at the contradiction that 'it seems that EULEX faces a very delicate situation in which people expect to see concrete results in terms of improvements in the Kosovar rule of law institutions whilst at the same time being very sensitive to perceived infringements on Kosovo's national sovereignty'.[66] At a later stage, the interaction of EULEX with civil society representatives increased, but many Kosovars remained highly critical about EULEX.[67] Moreover, there were strong differences in the expectations of Kosovo–Serbian and Kosovo Albanian citizens regarding EULEX (ibid). Overall, the critique on EULEX dominated. As an international NGO staff member noted: 'In the fall of last year (2015) I participated in a civil society consultation in Brussels organized by EPLO. It was on the future of EULEX, and people from the Kosovo civil society participated. EULEX is incredibly, astonishingly unpopular. That was the feedback from Kosovo civil society'.[68]

In addition, it proved almost impossible for EULEX to work in the North of Kosovo. Supported by Belgrade, the Serbs in the northern parts of Kosovo had, for quite a long time, refused to recognise EULEX, which downgraded the capacity of EULEX in the North – an extremely difficult starting point for the mission. However, Brussels had been reluctant to deploy EULEX in the North.[69] The effort of the Kosovar government

[62]Ibid., 12.
[63]Author's interview with Pieter Feith, 20 June 2016, The Hague.
[64]A. L. Capussela, 'The West's state-building policy in Kosovo requires a radical overhaul', http://blogs.lse.ac.uk/europpblog/2016/05/05/the-wests-deluded-and-ineffective-policy-in-kosovo-should-change/.
[65]M. Palm, Accountability and Effectiveness of CSDP Missions: The Role of Civil Society. The Cases of EULEX (Kosovo) and EUPOL COPPS (Palestinian Territories) (Brussels: EPLO, no date).
[66]Ibid., 11.
[67]Mahr, E., 2017, 'Local contestation against the European Union Rule of Law Mission in Kosovo', *Contemporary Security Policy*, http://www.tandfonline.com/doi/full/10.1080/13523260.2017.1407060.
[68]Author's interview with Michael Warren, Pax, the Netherlands, Utrecht, May 2016.

to control the North led to new violent clashes during the summer of 2011.[70] As a result, EULEX officials faced frequent roadblocks and threats and KFOR had to be deployed to re-establish security.[71] As will be discussed in the next section, the continuing problems in the North were the reasons for the EU to demand Kosovo and Serbia to start a dialogue about normalisation of their relations in March 2011. Again, in such a complex situation, the possibilities of EULEX to coordinate or collaborate with local actors were quite limited. It may be argued that EULEX could have done more and better in the North, but this would not be easy given the fierce opposition from Belgrade.

All in all, the experience of EULEX shows that it proved extremely difficult to coordinate the interests and agendas at the international, national and local levels. The interests and preferences of the different stakeholders that EULEX had to deal with (especially the Kosovar and Serbian governments) were often contradictory and highly sensitive since in most cases they related in one way or the other to the status issue. In this regard, Capussela argued that the main problem was not a lack of coordination with national elites, but an 'overdose' of it, and that a firmer position of the international community vis-à-vis national elites would be needed to overcome the challenges of corruption: 'Real change is only possible in Kosovo if the current leadership's political, economic, and military power is credibly challenged'.[72] This would imply a stricter and stronger role of international interveners, which would not only be resisted by national elites, but probably also by a number of civil society groups. In this regard, EULEX strongly relied on cooperation with national political leaders. That choice was even more visible in the Dialogue, which will be discussed in the next section.

The EU-facilitated Dialogue – A European method?

The aim of the EU-facilitated Dialogue between Belgrade and Pristina was to normalise the relations between the two sides, to promote cooperation, to help them achieve progress on their path to EU membership and to improve the lives of the people of Serbia and Kosovo.[73] The reason to initiate the Dialogue was the ongoing tensions between Kosovo and Serbia, which hampered the deployment of the EULEX mission (particularly in the North of Kosovo). The EU used its political leverage to bring the two parties to the table (despite the reluctance of the two sides), making the normalisation of the relations between Kosovo and Serbia a condition for the SAAs (that both countries did aspire). The EU also used the political momentum and made sure it had the international mandate to lead the dialogue. After the International Court of Justice (ICJ) had concluded that Kosovo's declaration of independence 'did not violate

---

[69]P. Feith, *Met het Oog op Vrede. de Ervaringen van een Internationale Crisisdiplomaat* (Amsterdam: Uitgeverij Balans, 2014): 259.

[70]Ibid., 258.

[71]Radin, 'Analysis of current events', 185–6. An agreement between Kosovo and Serbia on the integrated management of borders eventually mitigated the situation, although the agreed plan of December 2011 was only implemented in December 2012.

[72]A. L. Capussela, The West's state-building policy in Kosovo requires a radical overhaul (no date) http://blogs.lse.ac.uk/europpblog/2016/05/05/the-wests-deluded-and-ineffective-policy-in-kosovo-should-change/.

[73]EEAS, 'EU-facilitated Dialogue for the normalisation of relations between Belgrade and Pristina', http://www.eeas.europa.eu/dialogue-pristina-belgrade/index_en.htm See for the General Assembly resolution 64/298, http://www.securitycouncilreport.org/atf/cf/%7B65BFCF9B-6D27-4E9C-8CD3-CF6E4FF96FF9%7D/ROL%20A%20RES64%20298.pdf.

international law', High Representative Catherine Ashton declared that the future of Kosovo and Serbia lay in the European Union, and therefore, a dialogue between the two countries should be initiated. The EU's willingness to facilitate the Dialogue was mentioned in the United Nations General Assembly Resolution 64/298 which acknowledged the advisory opinion of the ICJ on Kosovo.[74]

The dialogue led to tangible results. In this section, we focus on the agreement reached on 19 April 2013, in which the two Prime Ministers finally reached the long-awaited agreement concerning northern Kosovo.[75] It was presented as 'The First Agreement of Principles Governing the Normalization of Relations', commonly referred to as the 'April Agreement' or 'the Brussels Agreement'. In 15 points, the agreement covered the governance of the Serb-majority northern Kosovo, where the Kosovo Serbs had continuously refused to accept Pristina's authority. Following the agreement, these municipalities were now to be integrated in the institutional framework of Kosovo.[76]

Indeed, the Brussels Agreement was another 'status neutral' effort to 'normalise relations' between the countries. The Dialogue was portrayed as a technical process, where it was clear to scholars, politicians and EU facilitators that a discussion about such different things as borders, political arrangements and trade would all touch upon the status question in one way or another. This 'hiding' of the political dimension was seen as a strength by EU facilitator Cooper, who – reflecting on the dialogue process – called this the 'European method' of seeking peace through practical cooperation.[77] Others, like Prelec, mockingly referred to the 'Brussels house style' of getting adversaries to commit publicly to an empty agreement 'whose content is to be filled in later, often by EU officials, out of the spotlight'.[78]

A detailed review of the dialogue process shows the sensitivity of the topics under discussion and the difficulties to reach agreement between the countries.[79] The Dialogue seemed to run aground on various occasions when the differences appeared to be insurmountable. The EU played a very active role in bringing the parties back to the table, suggesting new ways forward, while seemingly never losing its patience. Although for both sides the agreements signed were not easy to defend 'at home', it is fair to say that it was the carrot of EU accession that kept the Dialogue going and eventually led to acceptance of both sides. Moreover, the European External Action Service (EEAS) managed to mobilise international political support for the process. For example, when the talks had to be revived at the end of 2012, Catherine Ashton and Hillary Clinton visited Belgrade and Pristina together, expressing 'the support for Serbia on its EU path', and 'the objection of any kind of talks about Kosovo's borders'.[80]

---

[74]General Assembly resolution 64/298, 2, http://www.securitycouncilreport.org/atf/cf/%7B65BFCF9B-6D27-4E9C-8CD3-CF6E4FF96FF9%7D/ROL%20A%20RES64%20298.pdf.

[75]'Kosovo and Serbia Reach Historic Deal in Brussels', (13 April 2013) *Balkan Insight*, http://www.balkaninsight.com/en/article/kosovo-and-serbia-may-seal-eu-deal.

[76]A. Beha, 'Disputes Over the 15-Point Agreement on Normalisation of Relations between Kosovo and Serbia', *Journal of Nationalism and Ethnicity*, 43(1), (2015): 102–21.

[77]R. F. Cooper, 'The Philosophy of the Belgrade-Pristina Dialogue', European Western Balkans (2015), https://europeanwesternbalkans.com/2015/07/16/sir-robert-cooper-the-philosophy-of-the-belgrade-pristina-dialogue/.

[78]M. Prelec, 'The Kosovo-Serbia Agreement: Why Less is More', (2013), *International Crisis Group*, http://blog.crisisgroup.org/europe-central-asia/2013/05/07/the-kosovo-serbia-agreement-why-less-is-more/?utm_campaign=shareaholic&utm_medium=printfriendly&utm_source=tool.

[79]Van der Borgh et al, EU peacebuilding capabilities in Kosovo, 37–73.

Thus, the EU had a very clear idea of the outcome of the process and coordinated with a limited number of actors that had to be convinced to 'normalise' relations. While the Dialogue shows that the EU is able to facilitate negotiations, leading to increased cooperation between Kosovo and Serbia, it is also fair to say that the practical cooperation was primarily a result of the effectiveness of political pressure of the EU. In this regard, the EU showed its ability to play a 'diplomatic role' in managing to bring parties to the negotiation table that were not really willing to start a dialogue about the normalisation of their relations and the EU strategically used its leverage by linking the Dialogue to its other instruments (most notably the SAA).

But while the EU used its leverage to put pressure on national elites, it left out other stakeholders that had an interest in the process. The communication from the EU about the progress of the Dialogue was minimal, and the political leaders in Kosovo and Serbia were expected to communicate progress and results with their constituencies. The political elites in Serbia, and in Kosovo, had to 'sell' the deal at home. This led to contradictory messages sent out by political elites in Serbia and Kosovo on key issues (such as the nature of the future association in northern Kosovo) and to uncertainty about future developments, especially in the North of Kosovo.[81]

Arguably, these flaws were all part of the difficult process of reaching agreements in a complex and volatile environment and may be seen as a 'price' that had to be paid. However, the different stakeholders involved have different views about the achievement and the price paid for it. Moreover, the dialogue process also led to new fault lines in Kosovo and Serbia between political parties that either resisted or supported the process and agreements. In the North of Kosovo, the agreement intensified the intra-ethnic split.[82] In Kosovo, the consequences of the Dialogue for Kosovar statehood were hotly debated in society, leading to escalation in parliament where the opposition used tear gas and laser pointers against the defenders of the deal in the Kosovar parliament.[83] Another result of the agreement was the growing influence of Belgrade in the North of Kosovo, where the Kosovo Serb leaders disagreed with the deal and the government of Serbia to put together a political party 'Srpska Lista' that operated in line with Belgrade's political stance.[84]

The dialogue between Kosovo and Serbia has further been criticised for a de facto change of strategy of international actors that placed less emphasis on rule of law reform (as promoted by EULEX) and more on hammering out a political deal. Bodo Weber noted that while there was indeed a need 'to put the dialogue first' in order to secure Kosovo's territorial integrity and sovereignty, the EU and the USA 'have underperformed in furthering democratization and the rule of law [and] have been

[80]'Clinton, Ashton Urge Serbia to Continue Kosovo Talks', (30 October 2012) *Balkan Insight*. http://www.balkaninsight.com/en/article/clinton-ashton-urge-serbia-to-continue-kosovo-talks .

[81]Van der Borgh et al, EU peacebuilding capabilities in Kosovo.

[82]R. Zupančič, 'A Bottom up Perspective on the Normative Power Europe in North Kosovo: the Social Psychological Implications for the Locals', *Contemporary Security Policy* (2018) (forthcoming).

[83]Kosovo parliament buys scanners to stop MPs bringing teargas to work, The Guardian, 16 March 2016, https://www.theguardian.com/world/2016/mar/11/kosovo-parliament-buys-scanners-to-stop-mps-bringing-teargas-to-work; P. le Roy, *Kosovo: a 'European' or an 'Albanian' State?* (MA Thesis, Utrecht University, 2016). file:///C:/Users/Chris/Downloads/MA-thesis-Puck-le-Roy.pdf.

[84]N. Stel and C. van der Borgh, 'Political parties and minority governance in hybrid political orders: Reflections from Lebanon's Palestinian settlements and Kosovo's Serbian enclaves', in Journal of Intervention and Statebuilding 11, no. 4 (2017), 490–510.

consistently trading democracy and the rule of law to concentrate their efforts on solving the status dispute conflict'.[85] While this view is not shared by all EU officials, few doubt that tensions exist between different EU interventions and that 'the capability to work in and across different policy domains' was put to the test in the case of Kosovo. It is equally clear that the view of *how* to work across different policy domains, how to sequence interventions and what a priority is and why was (and often will be) contested.[86]

All in all, the case of the Dialogue shows the EU's ability to play a diplomatic role in managing to bring parties to the negotiation table that were not really willing to start a dialogue about the normalisation of their relations, and the EU strategically used its leverage by linking the Dialogue to its other instruments (most notably the SAA). The EEAS also showed a capability to coordinate with international actors – in particular the USA – at the moment that the Dialogue reached its most difficult moments. But the dialogue process came at the price of excluding large sections of Kosovar and Serbian society. Given the contrasting views and positions about the status of Kosovo at all levels (from the local to the international), a more inclusive dialogue process may sound like a mission impossible, but it seems that the EEAS did not even try to develop more inclusive processes of multi-track diplomacy and seemed to believe that an elite pact was the only viable option. This choice came at the price of a lack of transparency and lacking popular support for the deal.

Conclusion

This paper analysed the capability to coordinate of the EU in two important interventions in Kosovo in the period after 2008. Particular attention was given to the capability – context nexus and the ways in which the EU interacted with a range of national and international actors. Intervention is conceived as a political process in which there is no pre-existing consensus about outcomes and actors need to construct a basis for collective action – a process that often involves intense negotiations.[87] The paper showed that tensions exist within EU Member States, between EU agencies, between the EU and other international actors and with local actors (national and subnational elites, civil society and citizens at large). Especially, the ongoing contestation about Kosovo's status at different levels (from the international to the local level) has greatly hampered the possibilities of the EU to coordinate different actors. However, the EU dealt differently with this challenge in the two interventions studied in this paper.

A major critique on the EULEX intervention has been that it was largely ineffective in terms of addressing organised crime and corruption. The complex international and national context in which EULEX deployed was certainly not helpful in this regard, but the claim of the ECA report that the 'special circumstances' cannot account for all the problems seems fair. The political nature of the task at hand was insufficiently recognised by EULEX. Not only had the mission to navigate between actors that held opposing views about the status of Kosovo, it also had to coordinate with the very

[85] B. Weber, *Progress Undone? Trading Democracy for Solving the Status Dispute in Kosovo* (Berlin: DPC, 2015), i.
[86] Whitman and Wolff, *The European Union*, 11.
[87] Colebatch, *Policy*, 26.

national political elites that were involved in organised crime and in corruption. EULEX' contacts and interactions with civil society could not compensate for this. Breaking the power of national elites would have required a clearer strategy of the EU and a coalition capable to implement that strategy. This would also imply a more explicit choice to include some actors and to exclude others in what Whitman and Wolff call 'a broad coalition [...] in support of an outcome-oriented process'. However, such a strategy would require a more intrusive role of the EU and would very likely come at the price of local stability – at least in the short term. The EU was not able to forge such a coalition, and if it would have been able, the question is whether it would not have been willing to pay the price of instability.

Interestingly, the EU-facilitated Dialogue had a much clearer objective (normalisation of the relations between Serbia and Kosovo) and a clear strategy how to achieve this. While both Serbian and Kosovar leaders were not keen to start a new round of dialogue and kept emphasising that they were not willing to change their positions about the status of Kosovo, it is fair to say that the EU pushed, if not forced, the two countries to join the Dialogue. The EU was quite successful in using the 'momentum' (the ICJ's opinion regarding Kosovo's independence), while the carrot of EU accession kept the Dialogue going and eventually led to acceptance of both sides. The EU played a proactive role in this process. It pushed the Kosovar and Serbian governments to reach agreements about the relations between the countries (without addressing the status issue). This was a highly 'exclusive' process with no involvement of civil society from Kosovo (including the North) and Serbia. However, this could not prevent that the process led to political turmoil in Kosovo and to political rearrangements in the northern part of Kosovo.

While it is understandable that international actors did not place emphasis on a more inclusive approach, from a WoS perspective, the question whether a broader involvement of local actors would have been possible is highly relevant. It would be too simplistic to argue that the inclusion of more stakeholders will lead to better results and that a WoS approach will be able to bring together the divergent interests of different stakeholders. However, a WoS reminds us of the need to involve a broader range of local actors, while recognising that inclusion brings new challenges. The opportunities and challenges of such an approach will always depend on the local context. But it seems fair to say that the EU failed to fully understand that local context and that a WoS approach would have led it to perform a more rigorous and dynamic evaluation of local society, identifying relevant stakeholders and matching these with its ambitions in different policy domains.

When it comes to rule of law reform, simply 'involving civil society' is not enough, and a combination of clear strategy and selective inclusion would be needed. International actors should recognise the deeply political nature of the reform process and the normative agenda that this entails. Corruption is a particularly interesting example of how a thicker engagement with different stakeholders (building a coalition with selected local actors willing to push for reforms) and an understanding of local processes could provide the EU with a more effective response. In the case of the Dialogue – an 'all exclusive' process, involvement of other stakeholders at different levels might have slowed down the process and would require certain skills of the facilitators. In a deeply politicised environment there is no guarantee to success, but greater involvement of local actors might have led to more support for the agreements and more sustainable outcome of the process.

Manoeuvring wars, rebels and governments: the EU's experience in Sri Lanka

Georg Frerks and Toon Dirkx

ABSTRACT

This article outlines the engagement of the European Union (EU) with the conflict between the Government of Sri Lanka and the Liberation Tigers of Tamil Eelam. It analyses the EU's interventions through a Whole-of-Society (WoS) lens encompassing both comprehensiveness and inclusivity. Gradually the EU became a more articulated actor, attaining a certain degree of comprehensiveness. However, volatile conflict dynamics and hostile government responses restricted the inclusivity of its operations. An increasingly shrinking political and civilian space hampered its access to civil society. By default, the EU's approach became more circumspect and indirect. Only after a change of government in 2015, the EU's possibilities for constructive engagement improved. Adopting a WoS approach could have remedied some, but not all of the EU's challenges in the Sri Lankan context.

Introduction

In this article, we investigate to what degree a Whole-of-Society (WoS) approach was attainable for European Union (EU) interventions in the context of the Sri Lankan conflict[1]. The WoS approach was developed in the Whole of Society Conflict Prevention and Peacebuilding (WOSCAP) project.[2] It can be considered a prescriptive and normative ideal that pays attention to the role of local societies, to multiple relationships at policy level and on the ground, and a wide range of stakeholders in the conflict space. The term 'Whole-of-Society' refers to a set of ambitions of EU (and other) policy makers to work in a comprehensive and inclusive manner.

We first define the EU's growing role in conflict management and peacebuilding and outline some of the challenges intervening actors are bound to face in this area, including civil society and non-governmental organisations (NGOs). We then present a brief overview of the Sri Lankan conflict and the post-war period up to present (2018). We summarise the broader international involvement in the conflict after which we focus on the major EU policies and programmes carried out in the Sri Lankan context.

---

[1]The name Sri Lanka was only adopted by the country in 1972. Before that date, it was known as Ceylon. For consistency's sake throughout this text, we shall use 'Sri Lanka' also when we refer to events or developments before 1972.

[2]This project was funded under the EU's Horizon 2020 Research and Innovation Programme, Grant agreement no. 653866.

Based on the Sri Lanka case, the article concludes by highlighting the different socio-political conditions enabling or hampering a WoS approach. This article is based on literature research, 10 selected key informant interviews[3] in Sri Lanka in early 2016 and earlier work on Sri Lanka by the first author.[4]

The EU's role in conflict management and post-conflict peacebuilding

The EU is playing an increasingly important role in interventions in conflict and post-conflict settings. Though such activities are not new for the EU, its conflict management and peacebuilding policy and its range of instruments have become more prominent over the years as exemplified by among others the Common Security and Defense Policy (CSDP), the creation of the post of the High Representative of the Union for Foreign Affairs and Security Policy, the establishment of the EU's External Action Service (EEAS) and the adoption of the EU's Global Strategy in 2016. Major crisis prevention and management tools include the EU's diplomatic engagement, the EU conflict early warning system and conflict prevention, the instrument contributing to stability and peace, humanitarian aid and civil protection, election observation, EU support for mediation and dialogue, and sanctions.

However, in addition to its instruments in the field of the CSDP, the EU avails of a much wider set of instruments that can be utilised in its crisis management and peacebuilding work. For example, the EU is the largest trading block and largest provider of official development assistance. Jean-Philippe Scherer, Branch Chief of the European Operations Centre, states that

> The EU is gradually trying to synchronize all civilian and military instruments in a single inclusive approach. This combined effort, also called the comprehensive approach, aims to increase the efficiency of our response to the complexity of crises. The concept is continuously being improved and now promotes a better integration of local capacities and the early involvement of regional actors in the pursuit of solutions.[5]

The EU's policy on the comprehensive approach is laid down in the Joint Communication to the European Parliament and the Council. In this document, it is asserted that 'the EU has both the increased potential and the ambition – by drawing on

[3]The interviews used in this article are referred to in a footnote. They are dated and coded to protect the informants' identity.

[4]Georg Frerks has a long-standing record of academic work and consultancies on Sri Lanka. Part of the insights used in the current study is derived from earlier work by him and his co-authors. See especially Georg Frerks and Mathijs van Leeuwen, *The Netherlands and Sri Lanka. Dutch Policies and Interventions with regard to the Conflict in Sri Lanka* (The Hague: Conflict Research Unit, Netherlands Institute of International Relations 'Clingendael', 2000); Georg Frerks and Bart Klem, eds., *Dealing with Diversity, Sri Lankan Discourses on Peace and Conflict* (The Hague: Netherlands Institute of International Relations 'Clingendael', 2005); Georg Frerks and Bart Klem, *Conditioning Peace among Protagonists. A Study into the Use of Peace Conditionalities in the Sri Lankan Peace Process* (The Hague: Conflict Research Unit, Netherlands Institute of International Relations 'Clingendael', 2006); Georg Frerks and Chamindra Weerackody, *The economic and socio-political context of labour relations and the trade union movement in Sri Lanka* (Utrecht: CNV Internationaal Context Analysis, report submitted to CNV Internationaal, 2011); and Niels Terpstra and Georg Frerks, *Rebel Governance in Sri Lanka's 'Uncleared' and Contested Territories during the 1990s and 2000s* (Monograph submitted to the Gerda Henkel Stiftung, Utrecht: Utrecht University, 2015).

[5]Jean-Philippe Scherer, 'The EU comprehensive approach (ch. 1.3.1.)', in *Handbook Missions and Operations, the Common Security and Defence Policy of the European Union,* ed. Jochen Rehrl and Galia Glume (Vienna: Federal Ministry of Defence and Sports of the Republic of Austria, 2015), 43.

the full range of its instruments and resources – to make its external action more consistent, more effective and more strategic.' The EU's comprehensive approach

> covers all stages of the cycle of conflict or other external crises; through early warning and preparedness, conflict prevention, crisis response and management to early recovery, stabilization and peace-building in order to help countries getting back on track towards sustainable long-term development.[6]

The document further specifies that 'Comprehensiveness refers not only to the joined-up deployment of EU instruments and resources, but also to the shared responsibility of EU-level actors and Member States'.[7] The connection between security and development is a key principle in EU operations, while the EU responses also need to be context-specific. To enhance the coherence and effectiveness of EU external policy and action in conflict or crisis situations, the above-mentioned document outlines a series of measures and associated detailed actions.[8]

It is striking that the Joint Communication on the comprehensive approach only refers to issues at the EU or international level and has nothing to say about the local context or local actors. This is a salient omission, especially because the EU has specific policies and programmes dealing with civil society and a prominent track record of interventions in this domain.[9] Paffenholz recorded that between 2001 and 2010 the European Commission alone disbursed EUR 928 million to civil society organisations (CSOs) in support of conflict prevention and peacebuilding.[10] The emphasis on civil society is one aspect where the WoS approach can be of help as it explicitly argues for 'the recourse to the social contexts within which they [external interventions] are implemented, and with the aim of seeing complexity, within local society and in the relations between external peacebuilders and local society, as an opportunity to be grasped, as much as an impediment to effective outcomes'.[11] In addition, Scherer outlines a number of general challenges facing the EU's comprehensive approach: the first one is the different levels of internal and external coordination, including the need to maximise civilian–military synergies.[12] Shared analysis, common strategic vision and joint planning are here of the essence.[13] Scherer also mentions the 'difficulty to maintain a balance between the reaction to events and a coherent plan', and the need to combine rapid, short-term responses with long-term efforts and to develop transition strategies from CSDP missions to economic cooperation and development.[14] In our description and analysis below, we shall revisit the above ambitions and challenges of

[6]European Commission & High Representative of the European Union for Foreign Affairs and Security Policy. The EU's comprehensive approach to external conflict and crises, Joint Communication to the European Parliament and the Council (Brussels: European Union, 2013), 2.
[7]Ibid., 3.
[8]Ibid., 5–12.
[9]European Commission, The roots of democracy and sustainable development: Europe's engagement with CivilSociety in external relationsi,'Communication from the Commission to the European Parliament, the Council, the European Economic and Social Committee and the Committee of the Regions (Brussels: European Union, 2012).
[10]Thania Paffenholtz, 'Unpacking the local turn in peacebuilding: a critical assessment towards an agenda for future research', Third World Quarterly 36, no. 5 (2015): 867.
[11]Mary Martin, Linda Benraïs and Vesna Bojicic-Dzelilovic, 'Introductory article: Mind the Gaps. A Whole-of-Society Approach to peacebuilding and conflict prevention', this issue (2018).
[12]Scherer, 'The EU comprehensive approach (ch. 1.3.1.)', 45.
[13]Ibid., 48.
[14]Ibid.

the EU's comprehensive approach for the case of Sri Lanka and indicate what the WoS approach can contribute to dealing with these.

Challenges in conflict management and peacebuilding

The rich literature on conflict management and peacebuilding is replete with problematic issues, dilemmas and obstacles that complicate external interventions, such as those of the EU. It is impossible within the limitations of this article to do justice to the many academic and policy debates in this field. We therefore have made a selection of five issues that we deem relevant to our discussion of the Sri Lankan case.

The first issue refers to the capability to coordinate. Apart from the need to coordinate all EU domains, instruments and actors, the Sri Lankan peace process (2002–2006) was a highly complex international affair with four co-chairs of which the EU was only one, next to Norway, the United States (US) and Japan. In addition, Sri Lanka had many bilateral donors with their own agendas and priorities that did not necessarily align with the agendas of the peace process driven by the four co-chairs.

Apart from coordination or coherence among international donors, Paris and Sisk also highlight the need of organisational coherence among legitimate representatives from the host society itself, avoiding an overemphasis on capital-based elites.[15] In Sri Lanka, however, the role of national and grassroots NGOs in the peace process was very limited, apart from perhaps implementing humanitarian and development aid programmes. Moreover, important constituencies were left out of the talks such as the Muslims, the left opposition, (up-country) Tamil parties and Sinhala-Buddhist radical nationalist parties.[16] Here the WoS idea of a 'thicker engagement [that] requires identification of and systematic involvement with the breadth and diversity of actors which operate at multiple levels' would have been beneficial.[17]

A second related issue concerns local alignment or local buy-in. As Martin et al. state:

> The proposition underpinning the Whole-of-Society approach is that peacebuilding and conflict prevention will be more effective when conceived as processes characterized by social imperatives and interactions, and when a range of actors, actions and intentions are identified and taken into account. It suggests a way of achieving appropriate configurations of external and local resources, agency and initiatives.[18]

Though the conflict parties in Sri Lanka perhaps did not openly resist the peace process when it started, they had their own reservations and motivations. The peace process was made conditional by the international donor community, which proved to be counterproductive,[19] while the conflict parties simultaneously tended to believe that a military solution would be better for them than a negotiated settlement. In fact, in the course of time the Rajapakse government (2005–2015) became very critical and hostile to

[15]Roland Paris and Timothy D. Sisk, eds., *The Dilemmas of Statebuilding: Confronting the Contradictions of Postwar Peace Operations* (London and New York: Routledge, 2009), 309.

[16]Jonathan Goodhand and Bart Klem (with Dilrukshi Fonseka, S.I. Keethaponcalan, and Shonali Sardesai), *Aid, Conflict and Peacebuilding in Sri Lanka, 2000 – 2005* (Colombo: Asia Foundation, 2005), 37–58 and 70.

[17]Martin et al., *Introductory article*.

[18]Ibid.

[19]Frerks and Klem, *Conditioning Peace among Protagonists*.

the international peace attempts. Though the peace process was supported by a number of Sri Lankan NGOs and peace organisations, large sections of local civil society resisted the foreign peace efforts as being self-interested or partial in favour of the Liberation Tigers of Tamil Eelam (LTTE). These included the *Sangha* (Buddhist priesthood) and a variety of Sinhalese-Buddhist organisations and political parties and sections of the vernacular media.[20] It is very questionable whether there was throughout those years really a 'ripe moment' or 'mutually hurting stalemate' facilitating a successful mediation attempt and whether peace really constituted a mutually enticing opportunity, as conceptualised by Touval and Zartman.[21] It could reasonably be argued that some parties in fact participated in the peace process in order to spoil the international efforts, as elaborated by Stedman,[22] while again others acted as spoilers because they felt excluded.

A third issue concerns the potential role of civil society and NGOs in peacebuilding. Mainstream donor policy considers civil society and NGOs usually as positively contributing to post-conflict peacebuilding and reconciliation. This is also reflected in UN, EU and bilateral donor policies and funding preferences. Yet, there exists quite some controversy on the role of civil society and NGOs in peacebuilding, both in academic and policy discourse. Some observers feel that they have become too dependent on donors and are just instruments in promoting a Western donor perspective even to the degree that they may be even fully captured or coopted by donor interests.[23] Others feel that in situations of war there are good and bad ('illiberal') NGOs. The latter promote nationalist, extreme viewpoints that in fact endanger peace and promote violence and hate. Hence, care should be taken to distinguish between the different CSOs and NGOs. Further, war and post-war situations are often problematic for civilian action to take off due to a host of institutional, human resource and infrastructural problems.[24] Moreover, there is often a political environment that is hostile to civil society and NGOs which are not rarely suppressed or persecuted by powerholders and regimes that do not tolerate criticism or opposition. In these situations, it may be difficult or even dangerous to provide support to CSOs/NGOs. More recent literature on the 'local turn in peace building' suggests that local organisations should be cherished because they provide resistance to hegemonic peacebuilding interventions and discourses and can provide bottom-up alternatives.[25] The situation in Sri Lanka reflects to a certain degree all those dimensions. Most notably, during the Rajapakse presidency the room for manoeuvre for CSOs and NGOs had become increasingly limited.

[20]See Suthaharan Nadarajah, *Sri Lanka's Vernacular Press and The Peace Process, Part of the Sri Lanka Strategic Conflict Assessment 2005. 2000 – 2005* (Colombo: Asia Foundation, 2005).

[21] Saadia Touval and I. William Zartman, 'International Mediation in the Post-Cold War Era', in *Turbulent Peace: TheChallenges of Managing International Conflict*, ed. Chester A. Crocker, Fen O. Hampson and Pamela Aall (Washington,D.C.: United States Institute of Peace Press, 2001), 427–443; and I. William Zartman, 'The Timing of Peace Initiatives: Hurting Stalemates and Ripe Moments', *The Global Review of Ethnopolitics* 1, no. 1 (2001): 8–18.

[22]Stephen J. Stedman, 'Spoiler Problems in Peace Processes', in *Nationalism and Ethnic Conflict*, ed. M.E. Brown et al. (Cambridge, Mass. and London: The MIT Press, 2001), 366–414.

[23]Birte Vogel, 'Civil Society Capture: Top-down Interventions from Below?', *Journal of Intervention and Statebuilding*. 10, no. 4(2016): 472–489.

[24]Christoph Spurk, 'Understanding Civil Society (chapter 1), in *Civil Society and Peacebuilding: A Critical Assessment*, ed. Thania Paffenholz (Boulder: Lynne Rienner, 2010), 18.

[25]See: Roger Mac Ginty and Oliver P. Richmond, 'The Local Turn in Peace Building: a critical agenda for peace', *Third World Quarterly 34*, no. 5 (2013): 763–783; and Paffenholz, 'Unpacking the local turn in peacebuilding'.

A fourth issue refers to the footprint and dependency dilemmas of foreign intervention as described by Edelstein[26] and Paris and Sisk.[27] Though foreign aid and acknowledgement were certainly somewhat important to the protagonists, the real influence of the co-chairs of the peace process and the international community in general was in fact limited. It was certainly not enough to change the objectives and directions of the conflict parties. Whereas the LTTE soon became disillusioned with the peace process after they were banned from some relevant international meetings being listed as terrorists, the Rajapakse government succeeded in building alternative support among non-Western countries such as Libya, Iran, Saudi Arabia and China reducing its dependency on Western countries that were in its view propagating a pro-Tamil negotiated settlement. The extent of these footprint and dependency dilemmas arguably could have been diminished if an approach akin to WoS was followed where local actors and agency were more actively involved in 'co-producing peace' in an 'inherently interactive process animated by the resources, capacities and perspectives of both local society and external actors',[28] rather than imposing it from outside resulting in counterproductive outcomes.

A fifth issue relates to the difficulty of making or bringing peace when fighting still continues or is planned for. Though a ceasefire agreement (CFA) was formally in force in Sri Lanka between 2002 and 2008, it was marred by over three thousand registered violations, including violent clashes between the conflict parties.

A final issue concerns the intractability of the conflict. As Coleman et al. sum up, intractable conflicts are conflicts that persist for a long time, resist constructive resolution, take on a life of their own, become complicated and result in negative outcomes. They are deeply rooted and have a strong emotional core and associated conflict narratives.[29] Similarly, Burgess and Burgess call intractable conflicts 'stubborn' and characterised by irreducible, high-stakes, win–lose issues.[30] The Sri Lankan conflict could very well be called a classic example of such an intractable conflict, complicating any external resolution efforts.

A brief overview of the Sri Lankan conflict and international involvement

The Sri Lankan conflict has long historical roots, but was fought as an overt, separatist war between the LTTE and the Government of Sri Lanka between 1983 and 2009, when the Sri Lankan Armed Forces defeated the LTTE militarily. Earlier attempts to resolve the conflict, among others through the Indian Peace Keeping Force (IPKF), direct and indirect (international) negotiations and facilitation by the Government of Norway, failed. The conflict concerned a complex political crisis that defies a mono-causal explanation. Political minority grievances, competing ethno-nationalisms, ethnicised politics, failed nation-building, religious intolerance, bad governance, inequitable

---

[26]David M. Edelstein, 'Foreign militaries, sustainable institutions, and postwar statebuilding', in The Dilemmas of Statebuilding: Confronting the Contradictions of Postwar Peace Operations, ed. Roland Paris and Timothy D. Sisk (London and New York: Routledge, 2009), 81–103.

[27]Paris and Sisk, *The Dilemmas of Statebuilding.*

[28]Martin et al., *Introductory article.*

[29]Peter T. Coleman et al., 'Reconstructing Ripeness I: A Study of Constructive Engagement in Protracted Social Conflicts', *Conflict Resolution Quarterly* 26, no. 1 (2008): 3–42.

[30]Heidi Burgess and Guy Burgess, 'Intractability and the Frontier of the Field', *Conflict Resolution Quarterly* 24, no. 2 (2006): 177–186.

centre–periphery relations and South Asian power dynamics are among the factors mentioned as contributing to the genesis and escalation of the conflict. The war has caused over an estimated 80,000 casualties[31] of which 27,000 were soldiers from the Sri Lankan Armed Forces, while one million people fled the country, and some 800,000 people were internally displaced. Though the fighting has stopped with the defeat of the LTTE, Tamil political parties as well as several academics and NGOs argue that the political issues underlying the conflict have not been resolved. They also demand that the final phase of the war should be examined including alleged war crimes and disappearances.

Over the nearly 35 years since the start of the war, roughly four different phases of international engagement with the conflict and peace process in Sri Lanka can be distinguished:

A distant war: remote interest, remote control (1983–2001)

Though Western donors, Japan and multilateral agencies had some interests in Sri Lanka in terms of trade, migration, international cooperation and development, at the beginning of the war none of these could be considered a major concern. Limited Western interests, a rather mild political dialogue and the implicit or explicit Indian predominance in the region characterised that period. Indian involvement peaked with the signing of the Indo-Lankan accord in 1987 and the subsequent deployment of the Indian Peace Keeping Force (IPKF). Overall, however, the 1980s and 1990s were a period of relatively limited involvement of the international community in the conflict, as the Sri Lankan government resisted 'internationalisation' of the conflict. This only changed with the signing of the CFA in February 2002 brokered by the Norwegian government.

Engaging with the peace process (2002–2006)

The peace process starting with the CFA in 2002 represented a convergence of major domestic and international changes of orientation. At the domestic level, the two main parties – the United National Front (UNF) government and the LTTE – became receptive to facilitation efforts by the international community (however, for their own particular reasons), whereas international cooperation became increasingly geared towards the peace, security and development nexus in what has been dubbed as an era of liberal peacebuilding. The peace process and the more open stance of the warring parties in turn fostered the willingness of donors to get involved. Between 2001 and 2003, the aid received by Sri Lanka grew by 350%. In addition, the 2004 tsunami raised a lot of international humanitarian assistance. Aid had become more 'conflict-sensitive' and – at least on paper – increasingly attached to so-called 'peace conditionalities'.[32] At the Tokyo donor conference, for example, donors pledged an unprecedented US 4.5 billion dollars to support the peace process. However, donors stated as well that

[31]There are widely differing estimates of the number of casualties. Some estimates are significantly higher, especially due to the last bloody phase of the war in which according to some accounts some 40,000 people were killed. All estimates are subject to controversy.

[32]Frerks and Klem, *Conditioning Peace among Protagonists.*

'assistance by the donor community must be closely linked to substantial and parallel progress in the peace process towards fulfilment of the objectives agreed upon by the parties in Oslo' and that 'the international community intends to review and monitor the progress of the peace process closely'. To this end, they developed 10 'objectives and milestones'.[33]

In this period, the Sri Lankan peace process became internationalised in different ways: international security guarantees and an international Sri Lanka Monitoring Mission (SLMM) to supervise the CFA, Norwegian facilitation of Track One negotiations, a co-chair system overlooking the peace process with Norway, the EU, the US and Japan as co-chairs, international funding, support for Track Two initiatives and a donor reconstruction package.[34] It has been argued that there was in fact an 'over-internationalisation', and that the process was not only internationally *supported* but also became nearly completely *driven* by the donors.[35] This undermined the credibility of the process domestically. In any case, after about 3 years the process stagnated and a political solution increasingly got out of reach. Ultimately, the peace process unravelled without any tangible result.

Disengagement and critique (2006–2015)

After a new Sri Lankan government under President Rajapakse came to power in 2005, the relations of the government with the Western donor community turned into a much more distant, if not hostile, relationship. In 2007, President Rajapakse was able to regain military control of the East and evict the LTTE. After that, the tables turned against the LTTE. The government formally abrogated the CFA in 2008 to pursue a military solution to the conflict. A bloody military campaign with high military and civilian losses, initially against fierce LTTE resistance, led to the defeat of the LTTE in May 2009 and the complete extinction of its military and political leadership, including leader Prabhakaran. President Rajapakse claimed the total victory.

In the meantime, the Sri Lankan government had turned to countries like China, Iran and Libya for diplomatic, military and financial support, side-lining the Western donor community, as the latter had increasingly questioned the militarised approach of the government and its deteriorating human rights record. After the end of the war, allegations of war crimes and crimes against humanity dominated and soured the mutual relationship further.

Donor re-engagement under a new dispensation (2015–present)

After the surprising electoral defeat of President Rajapakse early 2015, there was a rapprochement between the Western donor community and the new coalition government under President Sirisena and Prime minister Wickramasinghe. The international community was relieved that there was a change of government and stood squarely, if not uncritically, behind the new government and its promised post-conflict policies.

---

[33]For details see: §18 of the Tokyo Declaration on Reconstruction and Development of Sri Lanka. 10 June 2003, http://www.mofa.go.jp/region/asia-paci/srilanka/conf0306/declaration.html (accessed January 02 2018).
[34]Goodhand and Klem, *Aid, Conflict and Peacebuilding in Sri Lanka, 2000 – 2005*, 72.
[35]Ibid., 74–75.

Below we deal in larger detail with the involvement of the EU, largely following the chronology depicted above.

The EU's involvement in Sri Lanka

EU–Sri Lanka relations are formally directed by 'The Cooperation Agreement between the European Community and the Democratic Socialist Republic of Sri Lanka on Partnership and Development' (1995). Cooperation between the EU and Sri Lanka used to cover a large number of areas, such as trade, investment, agriculture, fisheries, science, tourism, environmental care and many others, and could in that sense be called comprehensive *avant-la-lettre*. The agreement foresees Sri Lanka gradually becoming a partner in trade and economy instead of a receptor of aid. Strikingly, the agreement did not refer to the conflict that was already ongoing for over a decade, and included no peace conditionalities or clauses stipulating cessation of the agreement in case of violations of human rights or a failure to maintain democratic principles.

Diplomacy

In 1985, there was already some discussion within the European Community whether to come up with a communal declaration about the continued violence in Sri Lanka, but no agreement could be reached between the diverging viewpoints of the member states.

In the early 1990s, the EU carried out a démarche expressing concern about the developments and possible violations of human rights in the north and east of the country. In 1993 reference was made to the relationship between respecting human rights and democratic principles on the one hand and social and economic development on the other. In 1996, the EU rebuked the Sri Lankan government on the basis of 'principles of international law'. At the political level, the EU has issued several statements urging parties to engage in peaceful talks, while it also condemned the 'terrorist attacks' and 'indiscriminate acts of violence' of the LTTE. It has furthermore called upon the Sri Lankan government to lift the promulgation of emergency regulations. These actions remained declaratory and resulted in little concrete effect.

Contrary to its longer-standing interests in development and trade, it was only in the 2000s that the EU aspired to play a more prominent role in the arena of international politics and security. Possibly due to its limited traditional involvement in Sri Lanka and the absence of major direct interests, the EU has long refrained from adopting a dominant role. However, in 2002 the EU became one of the four co-chairs of the peace process. In this capacity, the EU stood out with its engagement with the LTTE, including advocating human rights. Contrary to the Americans, the Union kept the channels with the 'LTTE capital' Kilinochchi open, with Europe Commissioner for External Relations Chris Patten's meeting with LTTE leader Prabhakaran in November 2003 as the most salient example. In a series of (semi-annual) statements as a co-chair of the peace process, the EU reiterated the importance of the peace process, and emphasised the principles of the Tokyo Declaration. Over the years, those statements became tougher both in the direction of the government and particularly the LTTE. After the assassination of Foreign Minister Lakshman Kadirgamar, the EU tightened the screws on the rebels and on 31 May 2006, the EU listed the LTTE as a terrorist organisation.

Linking conflict and development

European development cooperation with Sri Lanka was initially directed at economic cooperation, which was to result in the reduction of poverty and the promotion of large-scale rural development, but later became focused on conflict issues, as we show below. The EU implements its bilateral programmes with Sri Lanka under the so-called Multiannual Indicative Programmes (MIPs). During the MIP I (2007–2013), the EU implemented three developmental programmes with a clear focus on post-conflict rehabilitation. The first of these programmes was the European Union Assistance to Conflict Affected People (EUACAP) that was launched in 2009 with a total budget of EUR 53.2 million. Its goal was to support the early recovery and rehabilitation needs of people in the North and East, leading to long-term development in those regions. The second programme was the European Union Support to Socio-Economic Measures (EU-SEM). The programme allocated EUR 15.7 million in grants for the development and promotion of socio-economic measures in the Eastern and Northern Province. The third programme was the European Union Support to District Developmental Program (EU-SDDP). The programme allocated a sum of EUR 60 million to support integrated socio-economic development in four districts in the East and North as well as some bordering areas.

Because of its relatively modest development budget in Sri Lanka (an annual average of between US 12 and 20 million dollars in the 2000s), the Union's aid leverage over the government was limited. During Rajapakse's reign, the implementation of the Cooperation Agreement came to a standstill, as the Joint Commission which under the agreement was supposed to meet annually had stopped meeting altogether since 2008, only to be resumed again in 2013.[36] During those years, the contacts were limited, as expressed by an EU official: 'We thought what are we going to do? We never spoke to them. There was no direct relationship with the government.'[37]

In the period between 2000 and 2015, 113 small and mid-sized projects were funded by the EU, mainly in the field of human rights, civil society and democratic participation as well as in conflict prevention and resolution, and civilian peacebuilding. Notwithstanding the modest size of most grants, they were experienced as very useful by the local recipients, if not indispensable to continue their work under the prevailing adverse conditions for NGO work during the Rajapakse presidency. A local Human Rights and Advocacy NGO that received funding under the European Instrument for Democracy and Human Rights (EIDHR) told us that the EU support had been essential, especially when the government branded them as 'Tigers' and was trying to make NGO work impossible. One of their representatives explained, 'Terrorism and the media were used by the government to diminish the work of human rights defenders. The regime argued that anyone who is not with us is a terrorist.'[38]

[36]European External Action Service & European Commission - Directorate General for Development and Cooperation - Europeaid, Multiannual Indicative Programme (MIP) 2014-2020 for Sri Lanka (Brussels: European Union, 2014), 2.
[37]In-depth interview with an EU diplomat in Colombo, 18 March 2016.
[38]In-depth interview with an NGO representative in Colombo, 15 March 2016.

For the NGOs concerned, the relationship with the EU had been very rewarding. However, the procedures and bureaucracy involved had been difficult for them to manage. This reflects experiences elsewhere, e.g. in Bosnia, where smaller and newer NGOs were effectively ruled out due to the complexity of the process and the requirement of matching funds.[39] In the Sri Lankan case, the involved EU officers and advisors had always been very cooperative and had helped the applicants to navigate the bureaucratic hurdles. The interaction in both directions was experienced as very valuable, as the EU was listening to them and had invited them for briefings. They also felt that the link with the EU and other local actors involved in those grants provided them with a level of protection.

The Centre for Poverty Analysis (CEPA) carried out together with the French NGO ACTED the EU-funded Citizen Report Card project that involved an extensive survey on free education services in the Vavuniya and Mullaitivu Districts. The involved government agencies generally cooperated well with the project, but sometimes the military would interfere with the fieldwork. This could be resolved in a reasonable manner however. An NGO representative said, 'Our staff interacted with the military and, you know, after some time they leave you alone.'[40]

Another NGO official was also very positive about the EU. 'I implemented seven EU projects. I am happy to work with the EU. They are the main donor here in the North. We did great things with the support of the EU.'[41] Similarly, an NGO representative who had worked on resettlement projects was happy with the EU support: 'The EU has been supporting the real needs of the community. It has had a big impact. Of course there are challenges in the implementation, but it supported the real needs.'[42]

A representative of an international NGO told that they had to manoeuvre carefully when dealing with the government. This interviewee explained:

> The Rajapakse government did not like human rights, governance, conflict prevention etc., …. The government has certain terms. They have a language, and we and the donors also have our language. If the government does not like human rights, we just call it human resources development. That does not change the project. When we write proposals I tell [our people] how to write the proposal based on the specific context.[43]

This was echoed by an NGO worker from the North:

> The terms that are used are important. Human rights and rights-based activities are very difficult in Sri Lanka. … [the government] feels that if there is a human rights project, that other countries see there is a problem in Sri Lanka. We need approval of government officers. That complicates human rights projects. … we could change it in "capacity building for local something", hahaha. So yes, we have to know how to change the terms.[44]

Another NGO representative explained they faced restrictions under the former government: 'There was a presidential task force (PTF), where NGOs had to get approval. We faced many difficulties. That is better now.'[45] Another informant also described the PTF:

[39]Adam Fagan, 'Civil society in Bosnia ten years after Dayton', *International Peacekeeping*, 12, no. 3 (2005): 413–414.
[40]In-depth interview with an NGO representative in Colombo, 16 March 2016.
[41]In-depth interview with an NGO representative in Kilinochi, 23 March 2016.
[42]In-depth interview with an NGO representative from Kilinochi in Colombo, 24 March 2016.
[43]In-depth interview with an NGO representative in Batticaloa, 19 March 2016.
[44]In-depth interview with an NGO representative in Kilinochi, 23 March 2016.
[45]In-depth interview with an NGO representative in Batticaloa, 19 March 2016.

> We always had to get approval of the PTF, we had to negotiate with the district administration and the provincial administration after that. … During that time the military asked several times to send progress reports to them. We also had a very bad experience with the governor of the Northern Province, a former military guy. … for even a simple project we had to meet him. He often said we could not work on peacebuilding; only visible projects such as infrastructure, housing, and so on. Even now [after the change of government], work on human rights is difficult. Colleagues working on disappearances still face problems with the military. … it is not sorted out yet. It takes time.[46]

These statements by key informants illustrate the difficulties NGOs encountered with the military and other government officials and how EU-funded NGOs tried and adopted a language that was seen as less politically sensitive in order to deal with or avoid the Rajapakse government.

In addition to the MIP I, the EU also supported Sri Lanka through regional programmes.[47] The regional programmes complement the bilateral interventions, mainly in the areas of aid to uprooted people, environment and trade. Between 2005 and 2015, the EU has contributed to the owner-driven reconstruction of over 20,000 houses for war-affected returnees through the EU's regional facility called Aid to Uprooted People (AUP) with EUR 50 million. The AUP programme further supported the World Bank who built 86,000 houses under the North and East Housing Reconstruction Program (NEHRP) between 2006 and 2009. The EU-funded NGOs Arbeiter Samariter Bund (ASB), Practical Action and ZOA promoted livelihood support measures and mainstreamed the use of local resources and appropriate materials.

The second regional programme SWITCH Asia has implemented four grant projects in the area of waste management, bio-gas and greening hotels. In 2014, SWITCH-Asia provided technical assistance to the Ministry of Environment to support policy development, implementation, monitoring and dialogue in the area of sustainable development.

The Asian Investment Facility (AIF) supports the Sanitation and Hygiene Initiative for Towns (SHIFT) implemented by Agence Française de Développement (AFD). AFD helps restructure the National Water Supply and Drainage Board (NWSDB).

The final regional programme entails Trade-Related Assistance by the EU. The EU delegation is preparing a project with the Department of Commerce of the Ministry of Industries to support trade capacity building and trade development in Sri Lanka.

In 2014, the implementation of the MIP 2014–2020 (MIP II) was launched. In the MIP II, it is stated quite honestly that

> The EU support to the UN's call on the government to firmly engage into reconciliation and accountability after the publication of the UN panel report pointing to serious violations of human rights and war crimes during the final phase of the war, and slow progress in implementing the recommendations of the 'Lessons Learnt and Reconciliation Commission' established by the President in 2010 have casted their shadow over the relationship between the EU and Sri Lanka in recent years. Only a few visits from high level EU and Sri Lankan officials took place from 2010 onwards, and the few areas of cooperation showing concrete results were the signature of an Aviation Agreement and the first meeting of the Committee under the Readmission Agreement in early 2013. Against

---

[46]In-depth interview with an NGO representative from Kilinochi in Colombo, 24 March 2016.

[47]Data on regional programmes based on a note on EU regional programmes provided by the EU Delegation in Colombo.

> this un-easy backdrop, the long term objective of EU assistance remains to help Sri Lanka to become a democratic, stable, secure and economically prosperous country, which should function according to the rule of law.[48]

While the MIP II characterises the current time frame in Sri Lanka as a 'post-conflict period', it also stresses repeatedly that the political and human rights situation is still precarious. It furthermore underlines that the current problems that Sri Lanka faces in the North and East of the country have the potential to cause discontent, unrest and conflict in the future. Policies in the fields of conflict prevention and peacebuilding therefore remain high on the EU's agenda in Sri Lanka. MIP II allocates up to EUR 210 million under the single focal sector of 'Integrated Rural Development'.

Under the new government of President Sirisena prospects for a renewed dialogue and cooperation between Sri Lanka and the EU improved and a variety of initiatives have been taken or are planned to be implemented. These included new development programmes and negotiations about a renewed application for the Generalized System of Preferences (GSP+)[49] that was withdrawn by the EU in 2010 on grounds of the government's failure to implement International Labour Organization and human rights conventions. The Council Conclusions on Sri Lanka of November 2015 take a welcoming stance towards the ongoing changes in the country, but also reiterate issues that require further attention, such as reconciliation, strengthening good governance and tackling corruption, promoting respect for human rights and the rule of law, and fostering inclusive economic growth and sustainable development. The document also refers to the required constitutional changes in view of political devolution and judicial mechanisms and an Office on Missed Persons to deal with the violent past.[50]

In order to support the developments in the country, the EU has funded 11 projects in 2015 in the field of human rights, democratic participation and civil society development under EIDHR and the CSO programme. The average size of these projects amounted to between EUR 400,000 and EUR 600,000.

Compared to MIP I, the EU has nearly doubled its development assistance to Sri Lanka to Euro 210 million for the years up to 2020 compared to the previous period (2007–2013). The EU will finance projects across a wide range of areas, including in support of the government's reconciliation priorities under the Peacebuilding Priority Plan, the resettlement of Internally Displaced People, assisting transitional justice and building local government capacity, as well as supporting development in Sri Lanka's poorest areas.[51] A landmark was the visit of the EU Commissioner for International Cooperation and Development Neven Mimica to Sri Lanka from 15 till 17 March 2016, to reaffirm EU support for the Government of Sri Lanka, review ongoing development

[48]European External Action Service & European Commission - Directorate General for Development and Cooperation - Europeaid, *Multiannual Indicative Programme (MIP) 2014-2020* for Sri Lanka.

[49]The GSP+ was the successor of the Multi-Fiber Agreement that stopped in 2005 and of which Sri Lanka was a beneficiary.

[50]Council of the EU, *Council Conclusions on Sri Lanka*, Press Release 820/15, 16/11/2015.

[51]European External Action Service, 'Meeting between HRVP Federica Mogherini and the Prime Minister of Sri Lanka, Ranil Wickremesinghe', European Union, https://eeas.europa.eu/headquarters/headquarters-homepage/12279/meeting-between-hrvp-federicamogherini-and-prime-minister-sri-lanka-ranil-wickremesinghe_en (accessed January 02 , 2018).

programmes and discuss ways and means of further enhancing Sri Lanka–EU bilateral cooperation. In a meeting with the Sri Lankan foreign minister, he discussed a wide range of issues, including the possible lifting of the illegal, unreported and unregulated IUU fishing ban and the restoration of GSP+. It was stressed that for this to happen, among others, human and labour rights issues would have to be resolved. The Commissioner also signed two new financing agreements.

Trade

Since then, progress has been made across a number of areas in bilateral EU–Sri Lanka relations, including the resumption of Sri Lankan fish exports to the EU in June 2016. The HR/VP welcomed Sri Lanka's GSP+ application, which would give the country preferential access to the EU's market. During a visit to Brussels by the Sri Lankan Prime Minister Wickramasinghe, the High Representative informed the Prime Minister of the state of play in the ongoing technical application assessment, while the Prime Minister committed to making additional efforts to implement Sri Lanka's international human rights, labour and environmental commitments, so as to give the highest possible chance for a successful application.[52] Both these issues have been resolved in 2017 after the EU declared to be satisfied with the progress made in these two dossiers. After the EU Parliament voted in Sri Lanka's favour on GSP+ concessions on 27 April 2017, the European Commission decided on 19 May 2017 to grant GSP+ to Sri Lanka.

Conclusions

Diplomacy and conflict resolution

In the early stages of the Sri Lankan conflict, the EU was not a very visible actor, like most other Western nations or international organisations. Sri Lanka was deemed to belong to the Indian sphere of influence and the Indians indeed took several initiatives in the 1980s, though with little success. In the 1990s, the EU became slowly more outspoken on the situation in Sri Lanka, largely expressing its view on Sri Lanka's human rights record and the promulgation of states of emergency by the Sri Lankan government. The EU also asked attention for the (humanitarian) situation on the ground in the conflict-affected areas and urged the conflict parties to engage in a process of peaceful conflict settlement. In those years, the donors had fairly little traction with the then government that opposed the 'internationalisation' of the conflict and rejected any attempts to help mediate the conflict. The EU's small footprint and the country's limited dependence on EU funding probably reduced the EU's impact. This suggests that normative approaches may be constrained by real political factors in practice. Moreover, the EU's attempts to coordinate the positions of the EU member states proved ineffective in the early years of the conflict due to the member states' diverging viewpoints, but later on this improved, especially in the field of human rights.

52 European External Action Service, 'Meeting between HRVP Federica Mogherini and the Prime Minister of Sri Lanka, Ranil Wickremesinghe'.

After a new, more receptive government came into power in 2001 and the CFA was signed in 2002, the situation changed drastically. The international (mainly Western) donor community wholeheartedly and perhaps uncritically started to support the peace process diplomatically, politically and with development funding. The EU was no exception and gained a more prominent role as one of the four co-chairs of the peace process. The EU allegedly helped keep the balance between the facilitator Norway, the more traditionally inclined Japan and the anti-terrorist US. The EU kept the lines open to especially the LTTE who was very sensitive to issues of 'parity'. The EU also communicated to the LTTE at the highest levels during the peace process. This shows that the EU per se had the required capabilities and prestige to act. When the EU proscribed the LTTE in 2006, some observers felt that this move endangered the whole peace process and the CFA,[53] though these were arguably already in a state of collapse anyhow by that point in time.

From our analysis, it can be concluded that, though the EU increasingly became a more prominent and active diplomatic and political actor, its room for manoeuvre was in fact determined by the warring parties and the stances of the subsequent Sri Lankan governments towards outside interference that varied from welcoming to outspokenly hostile over time. Neither the EU nor the other external parties involved had much influence over those dynamics and could do preciously little to change the state of affairs. This was partly caused by the intractability of the conflict and intransigence of the conflict parties. Another reason was that the peace process was not sufficiently inclusive and faced strong opposition by powerful local constituencies in Sri Lanka that actively tried to spoil the process. It even could be questioned whether the protagonist parties themselves were seriously interested in a negotiated settlement or tried to use the ceasefire to prepare for war.

In this context, the EU could in retrospect have benefitted considerably from adopting a WoS approach. Such an approach would have helped to avoid overlooking important local constituencies and leaving out local actors who thus became inclined to spoil the peace process. Also the WoS insistence on the 'co-production' of a peace process could have reduced the one-sided, donor-driven internationalisation of the Sri Lankan peace process at the detriment of local involvement and thus have contributed to local acceptance instead of the resistance it provoked. If the EU and the other co-chairs would have cultivated 'the organic interaction between multiple external and internal stakeholders, in so-called hybrid peace strategies',[54] as promoted by a WoS approach, such negative consequences could have been prevented. This episode shows that even when all powers and resources of the Western donor community get combined, these do not compensate for an initial lack of inclusivity and buy-in. Such a situation becomes difficult to correct once positions and perceptions have hardened.

---

[53]See, e.g., Jon O. Solnes, *A Powderkeg in Paradise. Lost Opportunity for Peace in Sri Lanka* (Delhi: Konark Publishers Pvt. Ltd., 2010), 108–113.

[54]Martin et al., *Introductory article.*

Trade: GSP+ and fisheries products

The EU is one the most important trade partners of Sri Lanka and forms its main export market. Though the earlier Rajapakse governments tried to deny this, there are no easy alternatives for this in the Asian region. The negotiations on the GSP+ and the recently concluded talks about the export of fish and fisheries products proved to exert significant leverage on moving the government in the desired direction in contrast to diplomatic efforts and development funding earlier. Here the strength of the EU's comprehensive approach is shown, as the EU successfully linked trade negotiations with progress in the fields of human rights, labour and environmental concerns. This in itself shows the strength of the comprehensiveness as elucidated in the WoS approach.

Peacebuilding, post-conflict reconstruction and development

The EU has contributed to peacebuilding and reconciliation activities through a number of smaller projects carried out by NGOs under the EIDHR and the CSO programme. Though the amounts involved for these NGOs have been relatively modest, the funding was experienced by the local recipients as very useful, nearly indispensable, for the type of work done and also the contacts with and support given by the Delegation were highly valued, especially in the period the NGO-sector faced a lot of resistance and obstruction by the then government.

The EU has carried out a consistent and relevant post-conflict reconstruction and development programme focused largely on the needs of the conflict-affected areas. Its MIPs have been complemented by regional programmes and special instruments into a fairly coherent and conflict-sensitive set of instruments. It successfully linked development and conflict in both its larger and smaller programmes, showing the virtue of comprehensiveness as propagated in the WoS approach. After a difficult period under the Rajapakse presidency during which the relationship came to a virtual complete standstill, the EU–Sri Lanka cooperation got momentum again since early 2015, with the size of the development programme increasing considerably compared to earlier. Together with major donors like the Asian Development Bank, Japan and the World Bank, the EU is becoming one of Sri Lanka's foremost partners in post-conflict reconstruction and development.

All in all, it can be concluded that the EU has become a more articulated donor vis-à-vis Sri Lanka as a country in conflict or – as of more recent – a country in post-conflict transition. It has adapted its programmes, made them conditional and conflict-sensitive, withheld trade preferences and argued for human rights, peace, reconciliation and good governance. However, its room for manoeuvre was at the same time determined by a variety of local actors and dynamics and this proved to be an unpredictable and volatile experience leading to setbacks and outright failures, like the internationally supported peace process. It appeared impossible to maintain traction with subsequent governments or the LTTE, while important local constituencies were left out. The limited footprint, the intractability of the conflict, the lack of local buy-in, the spoiler behaviour of important constituencies and of the protagonist parties themselves all were complicating factors overwhelming the donor community, including the EU.

Returning to the WoS lens, the EU has over the years managed to use its large repertoire of instruments fairly well in the Sri Lankan case, thereby attaining the comprehensiveness it pursues. It must be noted that this was only achieved later in the course of the conflict and hence there was no comprehensiveness over the conflict cycle from beginning to end, as the EU aspires. In terms of inclusivity, the EU was able to reach and effectively support the small group of local NGOs that it funded, but was unable to overcome the shrinking humanitarian and civilian space in society at large as a consequence of adversarial government policies. At that point, even all the resources and power of the international donor community, including the EU, proved unable to overcome this resistance and adverse conditions. Also a WoS approach would probably have been unable to change this much. On the other hand, this was the result of what the government of Sri Lanka perceived to be a one-sided, top-down and partial peace process. It remains of course an unanswered question whether a more inclusive, bottom-up, localised and interactive peace process, as propagated by the WoS approach, would have resulted in a different outcome. Looking at the tragic end of the war in Sri Lanka, it would at least have been worth the effort.

Disclosure statement

No potential conflict of interest was reported by the authors.

Funding

This work was supported by the EU's Horizon 2020 Research and Innovation Programme, Grant agreement [653866].

ORCID

Toon Dirkx http://orcid.org/0000-0002-9358-0280

Index

Note: *Italic* page numbers refer to figures and page numbers followed by "n" denote footnotes.